ST?

A New Pentecost?

LÉON JOSEPH CARDINAL SUENENS

TRANSLATED BY FRANCIS MARTIN

*"O Holy Spirit, renew your wonders in this our day,
as by a new Pentecost."*
POPE JOHN XXIII

"The first need of the Church is always to live Pentecost."
POPE PAUL VI

DARTON, LONGMAN & TODD
London

First Published in Great Britain in 1975
by Darton, Longman and Todd Ltd
85 Gloucester Road, London SW7 4SU

Original Edition: *Une Nouvelle Pentecôte?*
© Desclée de Brouwer 1974

This translation © The Seabury Press, Inc.

Revisions in the text made by the author after
the English translation

Printed in Great Britain by litho by The Anchor Press Ltd
and bound by Wm Brendon & Son Ltd
both of Tiptree, Essex

ISBN 0 232 51334 1 (paper)
ISBN 0 232 51335 X (cased)

231.3

Contents

Preface

Pessimism and a sense of defeat are in vogue today. Even Christians disseminate gloom, though this be the negation of everything they are presumed to believe. A real Christian is a man of hope. St. Peter went so far as to say that a disciple of Christ should always have his answer ready for people who ask him the reason for the hope that is his (1 Pt. 3, 15). Hope is a component factor of our very being. However, nowadays, in certain quarters, it has a bad press. People are suspicious that hope is just a sort of tranquilizer or excuse, a distraction which diverts our attention from facing the problems which beset us.

CHRISTIANITY MEANS HOPE.

We have to take hold of hope once again and restore it to its rightful place, and this for a fundamental reason: hope is today, as always, a theological virtue. This means that it is a dynamic reality within us which derives from God and relies on God—God alone. Hope makes mockery of our weighty statistics, our probability charts, our prognostications about the future; it goes its own way despite our forecasts: "Your thoughts, says God, are not my thoughts, and my ways are not yours" (Is. 55, 8). Hope is the servant of God, the "Master of the impossible" who draws straight with crooked lines. Despite disconcerting setbacks, God leads all things for the good of those who love him (see Rom. 8, 28). Hope is the daughter of a God who refuses to be categorized and who knows how to overcome obstacles by making them his servants.

To those who at this moment are distressed because they cannot recognize—in the confusion and the changes of today—the Church of their childhood or even that of yesterday, this book offers a message: be of courage, the power of the Holy Spirit is at work deep within the heart of his Church, breathing into it a fresh youthfulness. It is the Spirit who is our living hope for the future.

When Vatican II was announced, hopes were high. Just before the Council opened, Pope John XXIII suggested that we should read the Acts of the Apostles and relive the time when the disciples were together in the upper room preparing to receive the Spirit, "joined in continuous prayer, along with several women, including Mary the mother of Jesus . . ." (Acts 1, 14). Pope John prayed and asked the Lord: "Renew your wonders in this our day give us a new Pentecost."

The Council came, and it was an inestimable grace. It opened new vistas and charted fresh ways for renewing the Church, but it entrusted to the future the task of bringing to full fruition the consequences of the logic implied in the Council's fundamental decrees. The Fathers at the Council were not unaware that the work which remained exceeded men's capacities to realize it, and they said so clearly: "The Spirit endows and directs the Church with various gifts, both hierarchical and charismatic, and adorns her with the fruits of his grace (cf. Eph. 4, 11–12; 1 Cor. 12, 4; Gal. 5, 22). By the power of the Gospel he makes the Church grow, perpetually renews her, and leads her to perfect union with her Spouse." [1]

We should reflect on these words. We must look to the Spirit beyond men and their limitations. Future historians will say that the Council opened a few windows in the upper room and let in the first breeze of springtime. But they will add, no doubt, that the "mighty wind" of

Pentecost had yet to fill "the whole house" in which the disciples were sitting.

We should not be surprised, then, that Pope Paul VI in his turn took up the prayer of John XXIII and asked the Lord to grant us a "new Pentecost." He has expressed this wish insistently and frequently, saying that the Church today needs first and foremost the miracle of Pentecost: the wind and fire and spiritual power which is the Holy Spirit.

The Councils, important though they may be, are but moments in the long history of the Church, and they leave their mark on that history at varying depths. The Holy Spirit has other ways and means of renewal. As the centuries go by, the Spirit, suddenly and without warning, releases a gulfstream of graces through the action of some saint who towers over his contemporaries: Francis, Dominic, Catherine of Sienna, Ignatius, Teresa of Avila; these and many more are living, radiant witnesses of the presence of the Spirit within the Church at moments of crisis.

Faith teaches us that suffering is the seed of life. It is perfectly normal, then, that the sufferings of the Church at this moment should give rise to great hope: no day was ever so pregnant with hope for the future as was Good Friday. Pascal was not afraid to write: "It is a happy time for the Church when she is sustained by nothing other than God." [2] This same thought is taken up by Father Caffarel when he says: "The hour of suffering is the hour of God. The situation is hopeless: this, then, is the hour for hoping. . . . When we have reasons for hoping then we rely on those reasons." He tells us we should rely "not on reasons, but on a promise—a promise given by God. . . . We must admit that we are lost, surrender ourselves as lost, and praise the Lord who saves us." [3]

This present moment invites us to discard our "reasons" for hoping; to put aside our easy optimism, our all too human strategies; to nourish our hope at its source—the word of God. Everything points to the fact that we are living at a turning point in the history of the Church, in which the Holy Spirit is revealing, to a degree unknown before, a mystery of death and resurrection. Now is the time to listen, in silence, with all our heart to "what the Spirit is saying to the Churches" (Rev. 2, 29). He is telling us, it seems, to carry out the ever necessary reform of structures. But beyond this institutional "overhaul" at every level—indeed, to assure its realization—he is inaugurating a spiritual renewal of exceptional richness. The pages which follow are an attempt to highlight some of the signs of this renewal and to discern the future to which they point.

I agree with the words spoken by the Patriarch Athenagoras: "The world today is giving birth, and birth is always accompanied by hope. We view this present situation with a great christian hope and a deep sense of our responsibility for the kind of world that will be born of this travail. This is the hour of the Church: united, it must offer to this world being born, some Christian orientations as to its future." [4]

When he was visiting me once in Malines, Dan Herr, the editor of *The Critic*, asked me: "Why are you a man of hope, despite the confusion in which we find ourselves today?" I answered: "Because I believe in the Holy Spirit." He asked me to write him a letter to substantiate my answer. I complied, and he, evidently judging that what I said could be a help to others, published it on the cover of his periodical.[5] I quote these lines here, since they contain in a nutshell the message of this book.

WHY ARE YOU A MAN OF HOPE?

Because I believe that God is born anew each morning,
    because I believe that he is creating the world at this

very moment. He did not create it at a distant and long-forgotten moment in time.

It is happening now: we must therefore be ready to expect the unexpected from God.

The ways of Providence are by nature surprising.

We are not prisoners of determinism nor of the sombre prognostications of sociologists.

God is here, near us, unforeseeable and loving.

I am a man of hope, not for human reasons nor from any natural optimism,

But because I believe the Holy Spirit is at work in the Church and in the world, even where his name remains unheard.

I am an optimist because I believe the Holy Spirit is the Spirit of creation.

To those who welcome him he gives each day fresh liberty and renewed joy and trust.

The long history of the Church is filled with the wonders of the Holy Spirit.

Think only of the prophets and saints who, in times of darkness, have discovered a spring of grace and shed beams of light on our path.

I believe in the surprises of the Holy Spirit.

John XXIII came as a surprise, and the Council, too.

They were the last things we expected.

Who would dare to say that the love and imagination of God were exhausted?

To hope is a duty, not a luxury.

To hope is not to dream, but to turn dreams into reality.

Happy are those who dream dreams and are ready to pay the price to make them come true.

Pentecost, 1974.

The Holy Spirit, Life-Breath of the Church

> *It is an essential characteristic*
> *of the spirit of our age, that a message*
> *makes itself worthy of belief to the*
> *degree that it shows itself capable of*
> *opening out to hope and to the future.*
> W. KASPER

I. WHICH CHURCH?

The word "Church" applies to a whole variety of images and models. It can be defined as a hierarchical society, the mystical body of Christ, the people of God, a community either local or universal, an eschatological community, the sacrament of Christ, a service to the world. A reason for our present tensions is that certain people wish to choose one of these models in such a way that it excludes or dominates the others. The truth is more complex: the Church is itself a mystery which opens on to the "ineffable riches of Christ," which we must accept in their totality.

When I was young, the Church was presented to us as a hierarchical society: it was described as "juridically perfect," having within itself all the powers necessary to insure and promote its own existence. This view reflected an image of the Church which was closely modeled on civil, even military society: there was a descending hierarchy, a uniformity which was considered as an ideal, and a tight discipline which extended to the smallest detail, governing the life of both cleric and lay person and imposing even upon bishops a whole series of bureaucratic servitudes. The list of things for which a bishop had to have recourse to Rome bordered on the unbelievable, extending even to asking permission to allow a nun in his diocese to change her will or a sick priest to say Mass in his room.

At the same time however, another vision of the Church was gradually taking shape before our eyes. My generation will always be grateful to men such as Dom Marmion, Dom Lambert Beauduin, Fathers Prat and Mersch—to name but a few—who taught us to read St. Paul in a new light and to discover the Church as the Mystical Body of Christ. Pius XII, in his *"Mystici Corporis Christi,"* beautifully highlighted this aspect of the Church's mystery which had been blurred for too long.

The Second Vatican Council emphasized the Church as the People of God on pilgrimage, at the service of the world. The Constitution *Lumen Gentium, On the Church,* took care in its first chapter, on "the Mystery of the Church," to multiply images of the Church so as to make sure we would not try to confine the Mystery of God within our own narrow limits. After this first chapter, the Constitution defines the Church, taken as a whole, as the People of God. This was to stress the priority of baptism and the radical equality of the children of God, and automatically implies a reform of the concept of the Church which we call today "pyramidal," thus situating ministry within the heart and at the service of the whole ecclesial body. The perspective became more evangelical and less juridical without however repudiating the role of the hierarchy.

I think the time has come for us, Catholics of the Latin rite, to set in relief the place and role of the Holy Spirit if we are to attain a more balanced understanding of the Church. I say "we Latins" because members of the Eastern Churches, both Catholic and Orthodox, have always strongly emphasized this reality. Paul VI recently recalled to our minds the need for a better understanding: "This too will be one of the most important and fruitful themes of the spirituality proper to the Holy Year: the Christology and particularly the Ecclesiology of the Council must be succeeded by a new study of and a new devotion to the Holy Spirit, precisely as the indispensable complement of the teaching of the Council." [1]

It is true that one can point to many places in the conciliar documents which mention the Holy Spirit. These were most often introduced as a result of the insistence of the bishops from the East or on the occasion of a debate on charisms. We still have to integrate fully the "pneumatic" dimension of the Church under its aspect of "communion in the Holy Spirit" (See 2 Cor. 13, 13).

The mutual acceptance of the Holy Spirit as a living reality, creative of the Church, will make it possible for unity to be established once more between Christians who remain faithful to the institutional Church and those who wish to be free from any organic link with it. We can already see an opposition, which increases as time goes on, between the great mass of Christians called "traditionalists" who continue to see the Church primarily in its visible expressions, be these hierarchical, liturgical, theological, or canonical, and a small group called "progressives" who look upon the Church as a gathering of believers engaged in a "search", who wish, moreover, to reinterpret the Gospel in the light of present experience with little or no reference to the "established Church."

Admittedly, our schema draws a line of demarcation which is much neater in its description than (thanks be to God) it is in reality. Still, these are the frontiers which we see being defined day by day, particularly on the part of our younger people who refuse to let themselves be "caught in the structure" of the institution, and who, unhappily, go further and further away from the Church or else look for unstructured and spontaneous groups within which to live out their ideals. This opposition is not a problem unique to the Catholic Church. It troubles and weighs upon the leaders of all Christian communities in proportion as these are structured.

The philosopher, Paul Ricoeur, a Protestant, declared recently that the solution of this conflict seemed to him to be among the most burning problems facing the Churches today. "Is it not," he wrote, "the most urgent task of those, whoever they may be, who direct the destiny of the Christian community, to maintain the level of this vital conflict and to guarantee for all a flow of life between the institutional and the non-institutional? For, today, the Church is on both sides. To recognize and to live this fact is a primary duty." [2]

More and more people agree that the great problem which the modern Church must solve is precisely that of finding the necessary bond between institution and liberty. But we do not have to invent this bond: it is not of human making nor does it result from an agreement we negotiate among ourselves. This bond has a personal name: the Holy Spirit. He, by nature, is the "bond of unity," the creator of communion: in every liturgy we allude to Paul's phrase which speaks of the "grace of Our Lord Jesus Christ, the love of God the Father, and the fellowship of the Holy Spirit" (2 Cor. 13, 13). It is the Holy Spirit who animates the entire Church from within, and it is the same Holy Spirit who gives to the Church the visible means and mechanisms of its structure. We will be considering this point in more detail throughout these pages. In this chapter it will suffice to concentrate on the various intimate and correlative links between "institution" and "charism."

II. THE TWO DIMENSIONS OF THE CHURCH.

Generally, in everyday speech, when the term "institutional Church" is used, one thinks of the visible Church, that Church which is there for all to see in its sociological complexity inherited from the past and in its diversity from culture to culture. It is "the establishment." Or, rather, this is how it is depicted by the mass media which usually presents it to the public in generalities, in images that are sometimes convex, sometimes concave, but preferably with a sensational and therefore misleading slant. And so we are viewing the Church under its sociological aspect, a tangible reality at the mercy of all contingencies. This is the Church which is alternately applauded and condemned, according to the political criteria of the moment, by politicians and journalists, in whose view the Church must be the ally of the government in power and the advocate of social conformity.

For the believer, the Church is a reality of an entirely different order. The Church is essentially and indissolubly a mystery at once visible and invisible, the mediator between Jesus and ourselves, entrusted with the task of making real the Gospel of Jesus and translating it for each successive generation. This Church of the Gospel is made up of individuals and is thus at the mercy of all the hazards of human weakness. But it is also enlivened by the Holy Spirit, clothed with his power and in possession of his pledge of fidelity.

The theological structure of the Church is one thing; the sociology of that structure, another. For the believer, the ecclesial community possesses an institutional order willed and initiated by the Lord, and this is forever bound up with the growth and vitality of a Church which is one, holy, catholic and apostolic. We can see this Church in outline in the Scriptures. There we find the first Christians faithful to the teaching of the apostles, assembled for prayer and the Eucharist, in a pluralism of many, diverse ministries, united in a brotherly community, guided by their leaders who are responsible for the good order within each group and the mutual relationships of the groups with each other; these Christians were loyal to the deposit of faith received and passed on by witnesses who were accredited, qualified, commissioned, and furthermore in continuity with the first witnesses of the resurrection of the Master. Such are the features of the Church as it was instituted, and they belong to its essence.

Even more than these structures, however, we have the history of the early Church to show us that at each step there was no disparity between "the organization" and the Holy Spirit: he was its soul and life.

The apostles received as their last instruction from Jesus an order not to launch out on their own initiative, but to wait for the promise of the Father: for him who would clothe them with power from on high and lead them into the fullness of the truth which they had just begun to glimpse. The "structured" Church is first and foremost not a juridical, but a sacramental reality. The Holy Spirit rests upon those whom he commissions. The first words spoken to someone who is about to go forth to act in the name of the Church are: "Receive the Holy Spirit." Even today there are no stronger words to be found than those used in the consecration of a bishop: "Bestow upon him, Lord, the ministry of reconciliation in words and in deeds and miracles." ("Da ei, Domine, ministerium reconciliationis, in verbo et in factis, in virtute signorum et prodigiorum".) These are not just fine words, they are an expression of faith.

The Church of the Gospel is, then, at one and the same time, visible and invisible. We cannot speak of two Churches, one visible and institutional, the other invisible and charismatic: the unity of these two dimensions is essential to the very concept of Church. As we view the Church in faith, we cannot set one in contrast to the other: a "spiritual" Church which is faithful solely to the Gospel and the Spirit, and an "institutional" Church which is more or less in the nature of an armed citadel.

This indissoluble union between the institutional and the charismatic was underlined by Pius XII in the encyclical *On the Mystical Body of Christ,* and Paul VI has returned to this point many times. Recently he declared: "Therefore all the institutional and juridical elements are sacred and spiritual because they are vivified by the Spirit. In reality, the 'Spirit' and 'Law' in their very source form a union in which the spiritual element is dominant." [3]

The word "charism" has become part of our everyday speech where it usually means something like personal magnetism or exceptional talent. In the usage of Scripture and Tradition (and this is the only usage that concerns us here), a charism is a special gift, a perceptible and freely bestowed manifestation of the Holy Spirit, a particular grace of God which is given for the benefit of the whole Body of the Church. We will consider this at greater length later.

It is well to recall here that our modern terminology does not always coincide with that of St. Paul. Some of the faithful see the words "charism" and "ministry" as being in opposition: they thus reduce "ministry" to apply only to those functions which are exercised regularly—for and within the community—by those who have been officially commissioned for this. But this misconstrues the thought of St. Paul for whom the word "charism" designates the most mystical and religious of the "spiritual gifts" as well as those visible functions such as apostolic preaching, teaching, and governing of the Church. Then, too, Paul insists that we look upon all charisms—and not only functions carried out by those in office—as ministries given first and foremost to serve the community.

I think we need to bear these points in mind if we are to avoid false dilemmas and pseudo-problems. They will help us not to separate "what God has joined together." We must never forget that the Church cannot exist without its charismatic dimension; to be deprived of this dimension would not be merely an impoverishment, it would be a negation of the Church's very being. The Church without charisms would not only be a Church missing a part of itself—like a man deprived of his hands—it simply would not be a Church at all: its very essence would be affected.

In western Christianity we have a tendency to describe the Church in christological terms and to consider it as a reality wholly constituted and given structure by Christ—to which the Spirit then comes to bestow life and movement. In such a view the action of the Spirit pertains to the second stage of building the Church. But this is false. The Holy Spirit, no less than Christ, builds the Church; it is not enough to think of his role as being merely subsequently to give life and unity. This does not mean, however, that there is some sort of dualism within the very heart of the Church's being: the Holy Spirit is the "Spirit of Christ himself" (Acts 16, 7), who was granted the power to pour down upon the apostles the Spirit which he received from the Father, when, after having suffered, he was enthroned at the right hand of the Father (See Acts 2, 32–33).

The consequences of this mysterious, interpenetrating action of Jesus and the Spirit has deep meaning for the life of the Church—for its spiritual and ascetic life, its liturgical and devotional life, and its apostolic ministry. The Church is the fruit of the mission of two divine

Persons: the Son who became incarnate, and the Spirit who continues his action of incarnation by uniting the community of believers to Christ, making them one in the Body of Christ and the universal sacrament of salvation.

In this same vein, hierarchy and charisms are not to be set in opposition any more than are the actions of the Son and that of the Spirit in the Church. The late ecumenist and Protestant theologian, Jean Bosc, has well expressed a similar warning in regard to separating Spirit and Word: "The Word alone always runs the risk of incurring a kind of sclerosis at our hands. Christ, imprisoned in our neat formulas, can become an abstract dogma, the Bible can become a dead letter, and the institutional Church can affirm its autonomy to the point of utter solitude. On the other hand, to isolate the Spirit from the Word is no less dangerous—that is, if I refuse to allow any dialectic between the two. This can lead to a kind of illuminism which invests the most human of thinking with enthusiasm. It can lead to deviations, movements which are all emotion and no content, or to a fascination with relevance which refuses on principle to accord to the Word any kind of permanence within created reality. If the champions of orthodoxy, who rally to the Word, deny the Spirit, the pneumatics who appeal to the Spirit for the justification of every form of spiritual anarchy, are no better. The history of the Church, both universal and protestant, can provide, one after another, examples of this kind of imbalance."

III. THE CHURCH LISTENING TO THE SPIRIT.

RECEPTIVITY TO THE CHARISMS.

Though it is true that these two dimensions of the Church meet at a deep level, it is also true that history shows us—and we should admit this—that there have been times of tension between the hierarchical and charismatic dimensions of the Christian community. Sometimes this tension results from the opposition of the hierarchy to pseudo-charismatic Christians. From the Montanism of the second century to some of the "Jesus Freaks" today— as well as quietism and certain false revivals during the intervening centuries—the list of pseudo-mystical or at least ambiguous phenomena is long indeed.

What bishop is there who does not receive regularly in his mail extravagant messages from some visionary or other? Counterfeits of the supernatural abound: it suffices to think of the syncretic spiritism in Brazil and elsewhere. Mass infatuation with pseudo-spiritual phenomena encourages one to maintain a cool attitude. Who in retrospect, would not sympathize with Father Peyramale and his bishop when they had to make a pronouncement one way or the other regarding the apparitions at Lourdes at the very time when an epidemic of false apparitions had just succeeded in troubling many souls? The gift of discernment is a very delicate one and the hierarchy is always strongly tempted to keep to the safest path. This explains, though it does not justify, certain wrong suspicions and condemnations to which history bears witness. Not infrequently we see that, at the beginnings of a spiritual movement initiated by a recently constituted religious order, there was tension between the founder and the hierarchy. Part of the history of the "exempt" religious orders results from conflicts of this type. Many founders and foundresses were at first, through misunderstanding, identified with certain illuministic currents of their day: one recalls, for example, the *fraticelli* and St. Francis of Assisi, or the *alumbrados* and St. Ignatius of Loyola.

We can think, too, of the intense suffering of a Grignon de Montfort who, in the eighteenth century, was successively deprived of jurisdiction in eight different dioceses in France, by authorities who were more or less jansenistic.

And there are extreme cases such as that of a foundress of a congregation who, expelled by ecclesiastical authorities, did not return to her convent until half a century later when, after her death, she came back . . . in the form of a relic!

SHEPHERDS AND FAITHFUL UNDER THE MOVEMENT OF THE SPIRIT.

I would like to make another observation which I think important: we should be careful not to identify charism and faithful, institution and official leaders. Charisms are not the prerogative of the faithful. On the other hand if we take the term "institution" in its broad sense to include all those realities in the Church that go to make up the principal structures of its tangible existence, and which belong to the heritage of its past, then the laity pertain to the institutional dimension of the Church just as much as does the hierarchy.

Each member of the Church is called to bear witness to his faith, both within the Church and outside it, and to actualize the potentialities conferred upon him in his baptism.

Neither laity nor hierarchy have an exclusive right to charisms. We could list among the "prophets" of our own age lay persons such as Frank Duff, the founder of the Legion of Mary, Mother Teresa of Calcutta, and members of the hierarchy such as Cardinals Bea or Cardijn, Bishop Helder Camara, or Pope John XXIII.

Neither of the two components, hierarchy and laity, makes up by itself "the institution." Within both, the heritage of the Church's past is present and living, and this includes the Gospel itself which is the witness of the faith at our beginning. Together, both must fashion their fidelity to the faith today, and both must confront the new realities within the life of the Church with the criterion of the Gospel. We constantly forget that the People of God do not possess as a correlative reality "the government," as is the case in the political usage of the term "the people." The term "People of God" refers to all the baptized, the Pope and bishops included.

Within the People of God, as the "pilgrim Church on earth," the pastors (that is, the shepherds) have a specific function to perform, a particular service to render. This service has to do with the visible unity of the Church. The shepherds are not appointed primarily to give orders, but to establish unity, to ensure communication and communion among people, to preserve continuity in time as well as harmony in space. A Church deprived of this guidance would inevitably degenerate into illuminism and individualism.

The pastors, since they are the decision-making organs of the Body, must be particularly attentive, in the Spirit, to "the signs of the times" and to the prophetic witness which arises on every side. They must learn to draw out these manifestations of the Spirit from their relative isolation and integrate them, under the higher authority of the Gospel, within the totality of the life of the Church, so that the Church may be a better witness to the kingdom that is to come.

There is in the Church a continual prophetic presence of the Spirit which is sometimes as loud as a clap of thunder, sometimes discreet. A prophet, perhaps, stirs consciences, proclaiming a message which strikes home, though it may be, at the same time, a bit one-sided. This is no reason for not listening to him. It is for the leaders to discern what is good, what comes from the Lord in his message, then integrate it in a larger vision which is, perhaps, more balanced.

We have a striking example of this in the Pastoral Constitution, *The Church in the Modern World.* There we see the teaching authority of the Church at its highest level, taking up in its turn and integrating within a larger whole a great number of prophetic appeals which pre-ceeded the Council, coming from laity and clergy alike, concerning major problems of our world: the family, economics, peace.

It is the Holy Spirit, then, who works within the shepherds of the Church so that their decisions truly conform to the Gospel, to the life of the Church, and to the coming of the Kingdom: and it is he who, at the same time, obliges them to receive and to obey the manifesta-tions of the Spirit which are always present within the whole People of God. And finally, it is the Spirit who constantly prevents the Church from considering itself as a final goal, and is a continual reminder of the Church's relation to the kingdom that is to come and to its unique Lord, Jesus Christ.

OPEN TO THE CRITICISM OF THE GOSPEL.

By a strange paradox, the Church, precisely because of its insertion into the successive historical context of each age, always needs to be reformed and subjected to revision so as to remain in steadfast fidelity to its unique mission. The Church, by its nature, is completely relative to the Word of God, and this radical submission means that it must constantly return to its source. The Spirit must always free the Church from its narrownesses, its compro-mises, and also its sins, for the Church is made up of human beings who are always deficient and unfaithful to the ideal they are called to serve.

Purifying criticism can come from without as well as from within; it can even come from adversaries. The adage, "It is right to learn from one's enemies," applies to the Church as well. Certain attacks made against the Church can be a call to an examination of conscience. The French revolution and the Russian revolution, to give two examples, questioned certain attitudes and actions of the institutional Church and pointed out grave sins of omission on the social level.

Criticism should also be able to come from within the Church. Moreover criticism which is constructive in spirit, which is inspired by love of the Church and takes a form that respects the norms of the Gospel, has every right to exist in the Church. Pope Paul VI did not hesitate to invite the members of the Roman Curia "to accept the criticisms that surround us, with humility, with reflection, and even with gratitude. Rome has no need to defend itself by making itself deaf to suggestions coming to it from honest voices, especially if these are the voices of friends and brothers." [4]

Authority owes it to itself to listen and to assume at times its proper responsibility when faced with necessary changes: it will thus avoid being relegated to rear-guard action. It is striking to see how the "children of light" can be so far behind the "children of this world" when it comes to accepting self-criticism and a strict and impartial evaluation of methods and results. Businessmen call in experts to hold a thorough enquiry into the workings of their organization and to point out technical or psychological defects, so as to eliminate anything which slows down or hinders the functioning of the company. I realize we cannot draw an exact parallel between the Church and a business concern. Still, there are principles that are applicable to any institution in which men work together to achieve a common goal. To accept and to foster critical examination is a part of the process of human endeavor that one ignores to one's peril.

The Church has, moreover, an abiding reason to question itself on the purely human level. It is not a society like any other. The message which the Church bears and which is the very reason for its existence demands obedience from those who are the representatives of the institution, as well as from the ordinary members.

A. Gesché, professor of dogmatic theology at Louvain, has made the apt observation, following R. Dulong, that one characteristic of the Church is that it is, first of all, in itself, an "institution-message". He writes:

"On the one hand, the Church is an institution which bears a message. This is not true, at least to the same degree of 'compenetration' of any other institution which simply attempts to organize an aspect of public life without aspiring to deliver a message. On the other hand, the Gospel is a message to be lived, not only on the individual level but also as a society, as a Church; and thus in some degree, in a manner that is institutional. For there will always be institutions wherever men aspire to live not only as individuals, but also as a body, the Body of Christ. The presence of the institutional dimension does not merely respond to some sociological necessity: it is the expression of a message which demands to be lived out communally." [5]

He goes on to observe that the Church, by the very reason of being an "institution-message," is a special kind of society which, more than any other, is committed to change. Precisely because its message does not change, the institution which must be at the service of this message, must itself continually accept the reforms that the message imposes. The institution can never settle down. Like the Son of Man, the Church too has nowhere to lay its head. The Church, living the eschatological tension, "strains ahead for what is still to come" (Phil. 3, 13). This means a continual pilgrimage, a continual setting out, which nevertheless does not invalidate certain fundamental structures that constitute and direct the order of its march.

Now that the ground is cleared and the terrain is firm, we are free to consider any constructive criticism which will help the Church be more faithful to itself, that is to Jesus.

It should be assumed that we take seriously the objections to the "institutional model" in which the Church appears to the world of today as of yesterday. There is always room for a periodic review of those things that make up the institutional dimension throughout the ages and in various parts of the world. This applies to religious orders and congregations, secular institutes, and charitable, medical, social, educational and apostolic institutions. In this sense, and at this level, we have nothing to fear by calling the "institutional" Church to account. The more the Church is evangelical and faithful to its origins, the more it will be true to itself and so be a more effective instrument of the Spirit.

This is not the occasion to consider all the objections made against the Church. They are variable and depend a good deal upon time and place. Let us recognize honestly that the institutional Church, as we have defined it, is largely indebted to its environment, as every one of us is. This can explain, without always justifying, that "weight of history" which encumbers its movement and accumulates extraneous elements which, like sediment, tarnish the true image of the Church. The Church must always step back from its history and look at itself in the mirror in order to see "the face it was born with," lest it go off and "forget what it looks like" as the letter of James warns us (1, 23–24). The history of the Church is for us a school of humility.

This same history is also a school of hope. There we learn that the Church's most disconcerting moments prepared the way for unexpected tomorrows. We now can easily think that we are at the end of the world when we are really only at the end of *a* world.

In order to appreciate this better, let us take one example of an unlooked for recovery arising from what seemed to be a disaster. Consider for a moment the history of Pius IX and the Holy See at the time when the Papal

States disappeared. The turbulent times of Vatican I and the entry of Garibaldi's troops by the Porta Pia into the pontifical villa are not so far from us, but what a world between us and 1870!

At that time, just a century ago, most Catholics along with Pius IX himself considered the existence of the Papal States essential for the structure and life of the Church. The Zouaves who died in the papal cause believed themselves to be defending the liberty of the Church. They were fighting for the independence of the spiritual power of the Church, an independence which seemed inextricably bound to territorial rights. To defend the Papal States was to defend the papal primacy and its plenary and free exercise. As a matter of fact, with the march of history, we have seen international law evolve and elaborate a statute which confers the full juridical recognition of international law upon institutions which nevertheless have no territory of their own. In those days, however, the volunteers who defended the Papal States against Garibaldi's troops did so with a religious conviction which remains admirable despite the fact that the historian of today can see clearly that the disappearance of the papal lands effected an undeniable spiritual liberation of the Church and of the papacy. The drama of that time was that people did not perceive a process of development that was not only inevitable but also spiritually beneficial.

OPENNESS TO THE LIBERTY OF THE HOLY SPIRIT.

The Church in all its dimensions obeys one and the same Spirit. As a visible reality of this world, it must have its laws and mechanisms. It cannot dispense with a code of law or with legislation, but it must carefully steer clear of legalism and a mechanical view of its own life. Canon law must always face up to the Holy Spirit and be obedient to his directions: the Gospel is, in the highest sense, the supreme law of the Church. The Word of God and the Spirit of Jesus are the ultimate authority in the Church and all hierarchy is at their service.

The danger of legalism becomes greater whenever the central authority attempts to elaborate, on a worldwide scale, laws which are too precise, with all the risks that that implies, since these must then be applied concretely in very different circumstances. There is always the temptation to strive for unity in the Church through the enactment of laws and decrees, but this is to confuse unity with uniformity.

The Patriarch Athenagoras put the Orthodox Church on guard against legalism when he said: "We have made the Church an organization like any other. We invested all our efforts in making it able to stand by itself, and now those efforts are expended in getting it to function. It goes, more or less, really mostly less, but it goes. Only (and he cried out—it was the only time I heard him cry out like that), it goes like a machine, not like something alive." [6]

This warning against the temptation to give preference to the organization over the organism was addressed by the Patriarch to his own Church. But it certainly applies to us Latins who so easily tend to look on things under their legal aspect.

I think we can see a similar attitude in Pope Paul VI. A few years ago, in a general audience, while speaking of the Church of the future, he said:

"We shall have, therefore, a period of greater freedom in the life of the Church and of her individual members. It will be a period of fewer legal obligations and fewer interior restraints. Formal discipline will be reduced; all arbitrary intolerance and all absolutism will be abolished. Positive law will be simplified, and the exercise of authority will be moderated. There will be promoted the sense of that Christian freedom which pervaded the first generation of Christians." [7]

To conclude this chapter, I shall present for consideration two texts which emanate from the Orthodox tradition. The first is written by Father Alexander Schmemann, professor of theology at St. Vladimir's seminary, New York and observer at the second Vatican Council. This is his reflection on modern ecclesiology.

"Ecclesiology is one of the great themes of our ecumenical age. And the first thing one must say about ecclesiology is that today it is polarized. It is polarized between the concepts of authority and freedom. One can say that the old presentations of *De Ecclesia* are coming to an end. As we know today, the classical *De Ecclesia* with its emphasis on structure, institution and legalism is the product of confessional polemics, of the great Western crisis of Reformation—Counter-Reformation. It is this *institutional* or structural reduction of ecclesiology that is being challenged and denounced today. Yet, as always happens, one extreme leads to another. When people tire of structures and institutions, they are quick to take refuge in a kind of illusion of freedom, not realizing that in shaking one set of structures, they prepare another one. Today's freedom will become tomorrow's institution, and so on *ad infinitum.* Perhaps it is time for us to realize that as long as we debate institutions and structures, and not the mystery of the Church in her depths, we are by-passing the real issue." [8]

The following is by Metropolitan Ignatios of Latakia and was delivered at the meeting of the Ecumenical Council of Churches at Uppsala in 1968. Bishop Ignatios invites us to recognize the priority of the Holy Spirit as the life-principle of the Church:

> Without the Holy Spirit, God is far away,
> Christ stays in the past,
> the Gospel is a dead letter,
> the Church is simply an organisation,
> authority a matter of domination,
> mission a matter of propaganda,

the liturgy no more than an evocation,
Christian living a slave morality.

But in the Holy Spirit:
    the cosmos is resurrected and groans with
        the birth-pangs of the Kingdom,
    the risen Christ is there,
    the Gospel is the power of life,
    the Church shows forth life of the Trinity,
    authority is a liberating service,
    mission is a Pentecost,
    the liturgy is both memorial and anticipation,
    human action is deified.[9]

The Charismatic Experience in the Church

Long before the Holy Spirit became an article of the Creed, he was a living reality in the experience of the primitive Church.[1]

EDWARD SCHWEIZER

We have shown thus far the harmony that exists between the two dimensions of the Church: the institutional and the charismatic. Now we should consider this latter more closely in the context of the Church's history from New Testament times until Vatican II.

I. THE HOLY SPIRIT, LIFE PRINCIPLE OF THE EARLY CHURCH.

"To each one is given the manifestation of the Spirit for a good purpose" (1 Cor. 12, 7). These manifestations of the Spirit, or charisms, are, as we have seen, gifts of the Spirit recognizable by their visible presence, and by their common goal within the community, namely to build anew the Kingdom of God. We see them shining forth on Pentecost morning, radiant as the first glimmer of dawn; moreover they continue to appear on every page of the history of the early Church.

A glance at the Acts of the Apostles provides an eloquent witness to this presence of the Holy Spirit. We are not singling out this particular inspired text in order to give it a special priority. We are aware that it must be read in the light of other sources and not necessarily vice versa. Nevertheless, the concrete examples mentioned in the Acts—this first history of the Church—are especially valuable.

From the very first page we see the Holy Spirit at work in ways that are surprising, even disconcerting. His interventions are numerous—some of them dramatic. It is he, clearly, who directs the course of events and moves the apostles and the community of the faithful. Moreover these interventions extend both to details in the daily life of the Church and to its expansion throughout the Roman empire—so much that it has been said in truth that the Acts of the Apostles is, in a sense, a fifth Gospel: the Gospel of the Holy Spirit.

Peter in his first sermon, as he stood outside the upper room on that first Pentecost morning, recalled to his listeners the prophecy of the book of Joel which spoke of this mysterious outpouring of the Spirit. "In the days to come—it is the Lord who speaks—I will pour out my spirit on all mankind. Your sons and daughters shall prophesy, your young men shall see visions, your old men shall dream dreams; even on my slaves, men and women, in those days, I will pour out my spirit . . . before the great Day of the Lord dawns" (Acts 2, 16–20; Jl. 3, 1–5).

Msgr. Lucien Cerfaux has described this scene in a moving passage:

"When the hurricane of Pentecost had calmed and the tongues of fire had disappeared, the ecstatic faces of the first Christians, aglow with a supernatural light, continued to express something of the mystery that had been accomplished. At the same time, their mouths 'prophesied' and sang 'in tongues' of the power of God. So it was with Moses as he came down from Sinai; so it was with Christ at the Transfiguration; so it was with Stephen whose face was 'like the face of an angel', and later with Polycarp and the martyrs of Lyons. The Holy Spirit is light and and he is wisdom. The Holy Spirit perfects Christians. Those first Christians in Jerusalem had lived with Christ and they remained 'imperfect', 'unfinished', until the day of Pentecost. It was not until then that they received their supreme consecration, but till then, they had been clumsily trying to copy their Master; the Spirit, on the day of Pentecost, finished the painting. Every now and again, we are told, Rubens would seize the brush from the hand of a pupil and over hesitant lines there would pass a breath of life. . . ." [2]

As we await the Parousia which will reveal to us the majesty of God, the Spirit is secretly at work. His presence can be felt on every page of the book of Acts more real and more active than the men whose names and deeds are recorded there. He is spoken of as a presence both beloved and sure. Even when Luke does not mention him explicitly we can discern traces of his presence, a "water-mark" on each page of the sacred text. The Spirit guides the thread of apostolic activity, weaves its secret course.

The Spirit of Jesus inspires the words to use before the Sanhedrin or the Roman proconsuls and governors (see Mt. 10, 20; Lk. 21, 15). And again, in preaching from day to day: "and in my speeches and the sermons that I gave, there were none of the arguments that belong to philosophy: only a demonstration of the power of the Spirit. And I did this so that your faith should not depend on human philosophy but on the power of God" (1 Cor. 2, 4–5).

The Spirit inspires boldness in the apostles: "The Spirit

said to Philip, 'Go up and meet that chariot'. . . . But after they had come up out of the water, Philip was taken away by the Spirit of the Lord and the eunuch never saw him again but went on his way rejoicing" (Acts 8, 29–39).

The Spirit gives strength to the martyrs: "Stephen, filled with the Holy Spirit gazed into heaven and saw the glory of God and Jesus standing at God's right hand" (Acts 7, 55).

The Spirit is present among the apostles; he is their life.

The Spirit brings Peter to the household of Cornelius: "Peter's mind was still on the vision and the Spirit had to tell him, 'Some men have come to see you. Hurry down and do not hesitate about going back with them; it was I who told them to come' " (Acts 10, 19–20).

The Spirit chooses those who are to be sent: "One day while they were offering worship to the Lord and keeping a fast, the Holy Spirit said: 'I want Barnabas and Saul set apart for the work to which I have called them' " (Acts 13, 2).

The Spirit is the joy and assurance of those who are persecuted: "But the Jews worked upon some of the devout women of the upper classes and the leading men of the city and persuaded them to turn against Paul and Barnabas and expel them from their territory. So they shook the dust from their feet in defiance and went off to Iconium; but the disciples were filled with joy and the Holy Spirit" (Acts 13, 50–52).

The Spirit presides over the decisions made in the new-born church—directives that will determine its long future—and the apostles transmit these directives, saying: "It has been decided by the Holy Spirit and ourselves not to saddle you with any burden beyond these essentials . . ." (Acts 15, 28).

The Spirit traces out the route to be taken by the apostles on their journeys, guides them and holds them back: "They travelled through Phrygia and the Galatian country, having been told by the Holy Spirit not to preach the word in Asia. When they reached the frontier of Mysia they thought to cross it into Bithynia, but as the Spirit of Jesus would not allow them, they went through Mysia and came to Troas" (Acts 16, 6–7).

The Holy Spirit directs Paul's missionary life in a special way: "And now you see me a prisoner already in spirit; I am on my way to Jerusalem, but have no idea what will happen to me there, except that the Holy Spirit, in town after town, has made it clear enough that imprisonment and persecution await me . . ." (Acts 20, 22–24).

Thus we see beyond any shadow of doubt how the early Church lived by, and expressed its faith in, the Holy Spirit.

II. THE HOLY SPIRIT AND THE IMPARTING OF HIS GIFTS.

The Holy Spirit reveals himself as a power, which sends forth the Church to the far ends of the world, endowing it with its missionary dimension, its catholicity. It is also he who creates the living unity of the mystical Body, making Christians holy, and clothing them with his power. St. Paul continually speaks of this omnipresent action.

Jesus had said that to those who belonged to him, the Spirit whom he would send would reveal himself by means of such graces and marvelous gifts that they would do greater works than he himself (see Jn. 14, 12). The charisms which mark in this way the life of the early Church, like buds in springtime, are essentially the varied and visible manifestations of a single unique reality: the life of the Spirit overflowing the souls of Christians.

The charisms are gifts conferred for the upbuilding of the Church, and they complement one another. St. Paul stresses this convergence:

"Now there are varieties of gifts, but the same Spirit; and there are varieties of service, but the same Lord; and there are varieties of working, but it is the same God who inspires them all in every one. To each is given the manifestation of the Spirit for the common good. To one is given through the Spirit the utterance of wisdom, and to another the utterance of knowledge according to the same Spirit, to another faith by the same Spirit, to another gifts of healing by the one Spirit, to another the working of miracles, to another prophecy, to another the ability to distinguish between spirits, to another various kinds of tongues, to another the interpretation of tongues. All these are inspired by one and the same Spirit, who apportions to each one individually as he wills" (1 Cor. 12, 4–11).

This passage along with the whole of the same chapter, forms a preface to Corinthians 13 in which Paul describes the unique glory and the fundamental primacy of love as a theological virtue which "does not come to an end." However, even if love rules over all, even if it is the sun of the Christian life, infused by the Holy Spirit, its light does not eclipse the splendor of the stars which also shine for us during the night.

For Paul, the Spirit of the risen Christ forms the eschatological People of God; he unites, purifies, vivifies and leads them into all truth. Despite the weaknesses and sins of this people, the Holy Spirit is, even so, the first fruits (Rom. 8, 23), the pledge "that we carry in our hearts" (2 Cor. 1, 22; 5, 5). This is why Paul speaks of the Church as the dwelling place of God (Eph. 2, 22).

Every Christian is a "living stone" whose purpose is a "spiritual house" (1 Pt. 2, 5); his body is a temple of the Holy Spirit (1 Cor. 6, 19), while Christians together make up God's temple where his Spirit dwells among them (1 Cor. 3, 16). It is not the role of the Holy Spirit to draw attention to himself; he glorifies and makes known Jesus and in Jesus reveals the Father. Nevertheless, we are aware of the action of the Spirit; it is like a breeze which we cannot see, yet the leaves quivering at its touch tell us it is there.

The Spirit is at work through and in all the abundance of the charisms (Rom. 12, 6; 1 Cor. 12, 4, 9, 28, 30 ff; 1 Tm. 4, 14; 2 Tm. 1, 6; 1 Pt. 4, 10). Some of these are extraordinary and striking, others are not. Thus Paul can speak of the gift of the word of wisdom or knowledge (1 Cor. 12, 8), the gift of faith (1 Cor. 12, 9), the charism of teaching (Rom. 12, 7; cf. 1 Cor. 12, 28; 14, 26) or of exhortation and consolation (Rom. 12, 8). There is the charism of service (Rom. 12, 7), the gift of discerning spirits (1 Cor. 12, 10), the gift of helping, the gift of administrating (1 Cor. 12, 28), etc. In Paul's mind the Church of Christ in no way appears as merely an administrative organisation; it is the Body of the living and personal Christ, animated by the Spirit of God.

III. CHARISMATIC EXPERIENCE THROUGHOUT THE CENTURIES.

Whoever reads the New Testament must ask the question: "Why is it that a like abundance of charisms did not manifest itself down the centuries?" St. John Crysostom asked himself a similar question and tried to answer it. He thought, he said, that the early Church had need of special treatment so as to sustain its missionary efforts and its exceptional situation. His answer is somewhat unconvincing. In fact, charisms, because the Spirit remains faithful, have never disappeared from the Church.

At the end of the second century, St. Irenaeus was aware of the permanence of exceptional charisms and treats them as common knowledge. Commenting on Paul's words that he speaks wisdom "with those who are perfectly mature" (1 Cor. 2, 6), Irenaeus writes: "The apostle calls those 'perfectly mature' who have received the Spirit of God and who speak in all tongues as he himself used to. So we hear many of the brethren in the Church possessing prophetic charisms and speaking all kinds of languages through the Spirit; and bringing the secrets of men to light for their good, and expounding the mysteries of God. . . ." [3]

Little by little, religious writing becomes more reticent on this matter. The perceptibility of the Spirit's manifestations within the ecclesial community lessened as faith grew weak and Christianity was more and more taken for granted instead of embraced as a way of life. Yet, although these manifestations were no longer evident on a large scale, they were still to be found wherever faith was lived intensely, as, for example, in the more restricted world of monks and nuns, especially in the lives of those who founded religious families in the Church.

In its beginnings, monasticism was, in fact, a charismatic movement. The asceticism which it extolled was looked upon as a victory of the Spirit over the obscure forces of the world, the flesh and the devil. The "Sayings of the Fathers" are filled with instances of the gift of prophecy, miraculous powers, especially the gift of healing. The excesses and naïveté, characteristic of a particular period, cannot hide the fact that the Christians of that era believed with a living and dynamic faith in the action of the Holy Spirit and in his gifts.

Many monks were looked upon as spiritual fathers, able to lead others in the ways of the Holy Spirit. To this day, particularly in the Eastern tradition, the Christian people continue to see monks as men who are spiritually wise and who can be approached for their advice and healing prayer.

Spiritual authors in general, when they treat of the charisms, are insistent that one should practice discernment of spirits with great care and consider such gifts not as ends in themselves but rather as means to enable us to grow in love. These authors, however, never question the fact that charismatic gifts exist. Throughout the history of the Church, except during certain times of reaction against sectarian abuse, the hierarchy has manifested a generally positive attitude. Bishops such as St. Athanasius and St. Basil relied on monks to foster spiritual renewal.

In the eleventh century, a well-known monk of Constantinople, St. Simeon, who was called "The New Theologian," spoke in accents that were undoubtedly charismatic. For him, Pentecost is always a present reality in the life of the Church; it is the Spirit who unites us to Christ and brings us to the Father, when compunction has revealed to us the way that leads to the interior light of the Holy Spirit. St. Simeon used to say that only those who have experienced the Holy Spirit, be they laity or clergy, are able to guide others.

If the West has a tradition in which devotion to the Holy Spirit is less conspicuous, still, the same faith is at work, particularly in the lives of the saints and the founders of religious orders. St. Ignatius of Loyola has written some classic pages on discernment, and his is far from being an isolated case. Both before and after him, theologians and spiritual authors reflected upon the gifts of the Spirit and gave directives as to their use. John of the Cross and Teresa of Avila might differ from one another as to the role in prayer of "consolations" and images experienced through the senses—Teresa's Christianity was more "human" than that of John of the Cross—nevertheless both of them lived the experience of God at its most profound depths.

To be aware of the presence of extraordinary charisms down to our own day, we should re-read the lives of saints close to our times. There was an era when it was considered beneficial, when writing the life of a saint, to accumulate instances of miracles and rare charisms. Then a reaction set in, and we can thank heaven—and the Bollandists—for the "pruning" that took place. Still, today we have gone to the other extreme. A careful reading of the lives of the saints—I am thinking of the Curé of Ars,

Don Bosco, and many, many others—will show the undeniable presence of charismatic gifts: discernment of spirits, prophecy, reading of hearts, healing, and other manifestations of the Holy Spirit. It cannot then be said that charisms belong to a bygone age.

IV. RECONSIDERATION OF CHARISMS AT THE COUNCIL.

It is common knowledge that the question of charisms was considered afresh at the Council. The occasion was an intervention made by Cardinal Ruffini in which he relegated charisms to the past and warned against overemphasizing them in a conciliar document for fear, as he thought, that the institutional Church would be endangered. In reply, I pointed out that the charismatic dimension was *necessary* to the Church. I summarized the doctrine of St. Paul, which I have presented here, and ended: "What would become of our Church without the charisms of the doctors, the theologians, the prophets?" I also took the opportunity of my intervention to ask the Church to believe not only in the charisms bestowed upon men but also upon women, and that we should invite some women as auditors to the Council, if only to symbolize our conviction.

In regard to charisms, the Council adopted an open and receptive attitude expressed in a balanced text indicating that, provided necessary prudence be observed, charisms should be recognized and esteemed in the Church of today. Indeed we might add: they are more important than ever before.

There are two principal passages in the Conciliar documents which treat of charisms. The first is in *Lumen Gentium*, the Constitution *On the Church*:

"It is not only through the sacraments and Church ministries that the same Holy Spirit sanctifies and leads the People of God and enriches it with virtues. Allotting His gifts 'to everyone according as he will' (1 Cor. 12, 11), He distributes special graces among the faithful of every rank. By these gifts He makes them fit and ready to undertake the various tasks or offices advantageous for the renewal and upbuilding of the Church, according to the words of the Apostle: 'The manifestation of the Spirit is given to everyone for profit' (1 Cor. 12, 7). These charismatic gifts, whether they be the most outstanding or the more simple and widely diffused, are to be received with thanksgiving and consolation, for they are exceedingly suitable and useful for the needs of the Church.

"Still, extraordinary gifts are not to be rashly sought after, nor are the fruits of apostolic labor to be presumptuously expected from them. In any case, judgment as to their genuineness and proper use belongs to those who preside over the Church, and to whose special competence it belongs, not indeed to extinguish the Spirit, but to test all things and hold fast to that which is good (cf. 1 Th. 5, 12, 19–21)." [4]

The same teaching on the charisms can be found in the Decree *On the Apostolate of the Laity*.

"For the exercise of this apostolate, the Holy Spirit who sanctifies the People of God through the ministry and the sacraments gives to the faithful special gifts as well (cf. 1 Cor. 12, 7), 'allotting to everyone according as he will' (1 Cor. 12, 11). Thus may the individual, 'according to the gift that each has received, administer it to one another' and become 'good stewards of the manifold grace of God' (1 Pet. 4, 10), and build up thereby the whole body in charity (cf. Eph. 4, 16). From the reception of these charisms or gifts, including those which are less dramatic, there arises for each believer the right and duty to use them in the Church and in the world for the good of mankind and for the upbuilding of the Church. In so doing, believers need to enjoy the freedom of the Holy Spirit who 'breathes where he wills' (John 3, 8). At the same time, they must act in communion with their brothers in Christ, especially with their pastors. The latter must make a judgment about the true nature and proper use of these gifts, not in order to extinguish the Spirit, but to test all things and hold fast to what is good (cf. I Th. 5, 12, 19–21)." [5]

The Council, by drawing attention to the charisms, has called upon the People of God to become more aware of the abiding, active presence of the Holy Spirit in the Church. These two texts are not unique; there are 252 references to the Holy Spirit in the Conciliar documents. And this same awareness of the Holy Spirit is evident in the liturgical reforms that followed in the wake of the Council. It is noteworthy how the liturgy, in its new prayers and formulas for liturgical and sacramental celebrations, has accentuated the sanctifying role of the Holy Spirit. In our next chapter, we shall reflect on this and set more clearly in relief the Church's living teaching, regarding the reality of the Holy Spirit's presence in our midst.

The Holy Spirit and the Liturgical Renewal

*The Church is founded at one and the
same time on the Eucharist and on
Pentecost. The Word and the Spirit,
the "two new suns" are inseparable
in their activity which reveals
the Father, and yet they are
ineffably distinct.*[1]

PAUL EVDOKIMOV

CHRIST THE LORD, AND THE SPIRIT.

Little by little the liturgical movement has allowed us to rediscover what is called the "prayer life of the Church." Romano Guardini, one of the pioneers of that movement, once characterized this renewal by saying: "People are re-awakening to the sense of the Church!" We have emerged from an era of religious individualism which nourished itself too much on marginal doctrines; the Eucharist has regained its central place, its full scope in worship and in life.

In the Constitution *On the Sacred Liturgy*, Vatican II took over and integrated to a large extent, work already done by pioneers in liturgical renewal. But if we truly want to pray and live as a community in harmony with the deep rhythm of the Church, then we have still a long way to go and much to discover.

In the Decree *On the Ministry and Life of Priests,* we read concerning the Eucharist these magnificent words: ". . . Christ, through his very flesh, made vital and vitalising by the Holy Spirit, offers life to men." [2] We have to weigh well these words which express so wonderfully the bond between the Eucharist and the Holy Spirit, between the Passover of the Lord and the Pentecost of the Holy Spirit. Indeed, these words bring us to the very heart of all liturgical and Christian life.

The words may surprise some. This is probably because we are inclined to think of Jesus and the Holy Spirit as being somehow juxtaposed; we do not grasp clearly enough the indissoluble bond that links the risen Lord, glorious and alive, with his Spirit who perfects his work and renders it present to us. We should understand that the Lord acts in his Church through and in his Holy Spirit, thus fulfilling the promise of the Father. Of course we can put the accent now on Christ, now on his Spirit. But though the two remain distinct, they are not separate; in the concrete reality of the Christian life, they remain in the phrase of St. Irenaeus, "the two hands of the Father." [3]

THE EUCHARIST AND THE HOLY SPIRIT.

When we celebrate the Lord's supper, our attention is drawn toward the gifts that are placed on the altar at the offertory: the bread and the cup. However, our gaze should first of all be directed toward him who invites us to his table and who said to his own on the night of Holy Thursday, "I have longed to eat this passover with you" (Lk. 22, 15). He says the same to us today; it is the Lord who first desires to unite himself to us. He loves us first and invites us to his table at which he presides invisibly while, in his name, the priest presides visibly. The Eucharist is Jesus coming to be with his own, as they wait for his final coming at the end of time. The Eucharist is an act both of the Lord and of his Church; or rather, an act of the Lord *in* and *for* his Church.

But this act of the Lord is inseparable from that of the Spirit. For it is through the Spirit that the Master is truly in our midst, in a new sacramental manner. The Eucharist we celebrate manifests to us the Lordship and power of the glorified Jesus. But this glory, as he told us, comes from the Holy Spirit: "He will glorify me" (John 16, 14). Jesus is Lord in and through the Spirit. The Spirit makes the past of Jesus present, especially his passover, his victorious passage from death to life. The action of the Holy Spirit is not at the periphery but at the heart of our liturgical celebrations. His sanctifying activity is not only present at the consecration in the transformation of the bread and wine, but it also penetrates us as we communicate in the mystery. "He who eats this bread with faith, eats at the same time the fire of the Holy Spirit," said St. Ephrem.[4]

This profoundly traditional view of the Eucharist finds classic expression in the Byzantine liturgy. In the *anaphora* that bears the name of St. John Chrysostom, we find the transsubstantiation attributed to the Holy Spirit:

"Moreover, we offer you this spiritual and unbloody worship and we ask and pray and entreat: send down your Holy Spirit upon us and upon the gifts here present. And make this bread the precious body of your Christ. Amen. And that which is in this chalice, the precious blood of your Christ. Amen. Changing them by your Holy Spirit. Amen. Amen. Amen. So that for those who share in them they may be the cleansing of soul, the remission of sins, the communion of your Holy Spirit, the fulness of the Kingdom of Heaven, confidence towards you, and not judgement or condemnation." [5]

There is then, a sort of double *epiclesis,* an action of the Spirit on the gifts to be consecrated, and an action of the

Spirit on the Christian community who are to share in these gifts for their nourishment, deriving from them strength that will increase their love for one another. For the communication of the Spirit to the faithful is first and foremost the grace of an increase in love which, in God, joins us to one another. Immediately after the consecration, we pray in the second eucharistic prayer: "Lord, remember your Church throughout the world: make us grow in love. . . ." This is the ultimate reason why the Church, gathered together to celebrate the Eucharist, prays for the coming of the Holy Spirit.

There is a text of the sixth century bishop, Fulgentius of Ruspa, which expresses this truth with a rare beauty and depth of meaning:

"Because Christ died for us out of love, and at the time of the sacrifice we commemorate his death, we ask that the same love be given to us by the coming of the Holy Spirit. . . . Thus it is that all the faithful who love God and their neighbour, even if they do not drink the cup of the bodily passion, still drink the cup of the Lord's love. . . . We ask that the Holy Spirit come, not according to the substance of his immeasurable divinity, but according to the gift of individual love. . . . The Spirit is said to come when he is invoked by the faithful, in so far as he deigns to give or increase the gift of love and unanimity. It is particularly in this gift, I might say, that the Holy Spirit is specifically recognized . . . Thus it is that when the holy Church, during the sacrifice of the body and blood of Christ, asks that the Holy Spirit be sent, she is asking for the gift of love by which she may keep the 'unity of the Spirit in the bond of peace' (Eph. 4, 3)." [6]

Father Tillard, O.P., from whose article I have taken the text of Fulgentius, adds this paraphrase: "To affirm that the Eucharist is the sacrament of love, that it unites believers to the love of Jesus at his passover, that it welds together 'ecclesial unity', amounts to saying that it is the sacrament of the gift of the Holy Spirit. But we must not consider this gift as something static, as something just given; rather we must see there the sanctifying action of the person of the Holy Spirit." [7]

We should note that this sanctifying action does not just concern the eucharistic gifts; it extends to the interior dispositions of those who are to receive them. God's offer and man's receptivity meet in the one mystery of the Spirit's action. We see this accentuated in the Byzantine Liturgy in an echo of the text cited previously. Shortly before the communion, the priest holds up the consecrated bread and chants: "Holy things for the holy," thus recalling that the same act of the Holy Spirit for which we prayed at the *epiclesis* has made both the gifts and the people holy and united one with the other.

After this brief outline of the indissoluble bond between the risen Lord and his Spirit at the heart of the Eucharist, I would like to consider other aspects of the liturgical renewal which point in the same direction, setting in relief the nearness and active presence of the Holy Spirit in the Liturgy.

THE LITURGY OF THE WORD.

The first thing to notice about the liturgical renewal in this respect is the scope given to the liturgy of the word as an introduction to the eucharistic liturgy.

The readings from Scripture bring us, by the grace of the Holy Spirit, into close communion with God as he makes himself known to his Church in the rhythm of the liturgical year. This is the fulfillment of the promise of Jesus that the Spirit would teach us: "I still have many things to say to you but they would be too much for you now. But when the Spirit of truth comes, he will lead you into all the truth" (Jn. 16, 12–13).

The Church opens out before us the history of salvation. Beginning at Advent, it reaches its culmination at the feast of All Saints, taking in, so to speak, on the way—like two mountain peaks rising from a plain—the glorious festivals of Easter and Pentecost.

These passages from the Scriptures are offered by the Church to her children with all the richness and mystery that accrues to them as they are read to the assembled people during the course of the liturgical year. A special grace awaits us if we accept this teaching given by the Church, our Mother, to enable us to model ourselves more closely on Jesus and thus come to the Father. The Spirit is the source of these chosen texts; he brings their meaning to light and makes their message real not only for the community at large but also for each one of us in particular. To open the lectionary each day in a spirit of faith is to "keep an appointment" with the Holy Spirit. These texts upon which the whole of the western Church at least, will be meditating each day, should have a special priority for us if we wish to "think with the Church" and allow the Spirit to form in us "the mind of Christ" (see 1 Cor. 2, 16).

In the pages of the Old Testament and the New, God speaks to me today. I should therefore receive his words as I would the letter of a friend who shares with me all my cares, fears and hopes, who walks at my side, showing me the way. Yes, the Holy Spirit speaks to me through the texts upon which the Church meditates each day. If I cannot be present at Mass, I can take a missal and, in spiritual communion with the Church, converse with the Lord and enrich my day with his message. Each day we should let him mould us by his word, even as a potter moulds his clay. Mary's answer to the angel, at the Annunciation, "Let it be done to me according to your word" (Lk. 1, 38), shows us how to accept the everyday happenings in our lives. If in our Christian homes we were to read daily some lines from the missal, in accordance with the rhythm of the Church's year, it would bring God's blessing upon our homes and become an "unending education" in the Christian way of life. We would become more open to God and more in union with our fellowmen.

Our Protestant brethren owe what is best in their religious tradition to their daily reading of the Bible. We, too, must learn to listen to the word of God: "Speak Lord, your servant is listening" (1 Sm. 3, 10).

When a bishop is being consecrated, the bishop who consecrates him says: "Receive the Gospel and preach the word of God, always teaching with the greatest patience." [8] At baptism we all received a similar mandate. If the mission of a bishop is to be the authentic interpreter of the word, in the name of the Church, it is also true that all of us are servants of the word and bearers of its message. We ought to familiarize ourselves with Scripture so as to be at home in the household of Jesus and enter more deeply into his Spirit. Moreover, one cannot but rejoice to see so many Christians—their number is increasing every day—who share this bread of life which is the word of God: here, too, we have a sign of hope.

THE EUCHARISTIC LITURGY.

It is not only the liturgy of the word that has been affected by the reforms which followed upon the Council. In our Eucharistic liturgies we have new texts which are richer and more varied than ever before. We have four Eucharistic prayers in all of which one cannot fail to notice how the role of the Holy Spirit has been accentuated. We all know that one of the points of controversy between ourselves and our Orthodox brethren has been *the epiclesis* that is, basically, the place accorded to the Holy Spirit in our Latin mass. This problem, we are glad to say, has disappeared today, now that the Holy Spirit is emphasized in these new prayers, and his role profoundly described.

Let us take, for example, the fourth Eucharistic prayer. Let us meditate on the invocation asking the Father to send the Holy Spirit to perfect the consecration of the bread and wine:

"Father, may this Holy Spirit sanctify these offerings. Let them become the body and blood of Jesus Christ our Lord as we celebrate the great mystery which he left us as an everlasting covenant."

Following the consecration, there is a prayer asking the Holy Spirit to unify all who participate in this sacrifice:

"Lord, look upon this sacrifice which you have given to your Church: and by your Holy Spirit, gather all who share this bread and wine into the one body of Christ, a living sacrifice of praise."

The Holy Spirit, therefore, is at the heart of the Eucharist, in the consecration and the communion.

THE LITURGY OF THE SACRAMENTS.

It is possible to see in each of the sacraments the action of the Holy Spirit. I will confine myself however to reflecting on some of the prayers used at baptism, confirmation and the anointing of the sick.

Baptism.

To clarify the role of the Spirit at baptism, it is enough to read the solemn blessing of the water that takes place during the Paschal vigil. The Holy Spirit is spoken of as he who sanctifies the water of baptism. After a reminder of how at "the dawn of creation" the Spirit breathed on the waters, making them the "wellspring of all holiness," the blessing goes on to speak of the role of water in the history of salvation, in particular the waters of the Jordan in which Jesus was "baptized by John and anointed with the Spirit." Finally, we ask: "By the power of the Spirit, give to the water of this font the grace of your Son. . . . We ask you, Father, with your Son, to send the Holy Spirit upon the waters of this font. May all who are buried with Christ in the death of baptism rise also with him to newness of life." [9]

Confirmation.

There were many important changes made in the ceremony of confirmation as well. First, confirmation is preceded by a liturgy of the word in which the readings are centered around the mystery of Pentecost. There are altogether 37 readings about the Holy Spirit in the new lectionary. Then, too, because there is a close link between confirmation and the Eucharist, the new rite prefers that confirmation be given within the context of an Eucharistic liturgy and that those who are confirmed participate fully in that liturgy, receiving the body and blood of the Lord.

The bishop prays collectively over those who are to be confirmed, extending his hands over them and asking God to send down his Spirit upon them. Then, he signs each of them on the forehead with the oil of chrism, saying: "N., be sealed with the Holy Spirit, the Gift of the Father." [10]

Few of us today would understand the words of St. Gregory of Nyssa when he says: "The oil and the bread, each, after they have been sanctified by the Holy Spirit, contains his divine energy." [11] We do not look on the Eucharist as being impregnated with the action of the Holy Spirit, nor do we think very much about the blessing of the oil of chrism. Let us reflect upon a few lines from the rite in which the bishop blesses the oil of chrism on Holy Thursday:

"And so Father, we ask you to bless this oil you have created. Fill it with the power of your Holy Spirit through Christ your

Son. It is from him that chrism takes its name and with chrism you have anointed for yourself priests and kings, prophets and martyrs." [12]

The Anointing of the Sick.

The new rite for the anointing of the sick gives expression to a theology based on the action of the Holy Spirit. As in the blessing of the oil of chrism, so here, too, we have a treasure with which we are not as familiar as we ought to be:

> "Lord God, loving Father,
> You bring healing to the sick through your
> Son Jesus Christ.
> Hear us as we pray to you in faith,
> and send the Holy Spirit, man's Helper and Friend,
> upon this oil, which nature has provided to
> serve the needs of men.
> May your blessing
> come upon all who are anointed with this oil,
> that they may be freed from pain and illness
> and made well again in body, mind, and soul.
> Father, may this oil be blessed for our use
> in the name of our Lord Jesus Christ." [13]

In the actual rite of anointing the sick, the Holy Spirit is mentioned time and time again.

We find this moving prayer which can be used by the priest if he is himself to bless the oil of the sick:

> "Praise to you, almighty God and Father.
> You sent your Son to live among us
> and bring us salvation.
> Praise to you, Lord Jesus Christ,
> the Father's only Son.
> You humbled yourself to share in our humanity
> and desired to cure all our illnesses.
> Praise to you, God the Holy Spirit, the Consoler.
> You heal our sickness with your mighty power." [14]

The entire rite of anointing has been modified so that it be truly the sacrament for the comforting and healing of the sick: it is no longer called "Extreme Unction" or "The Last Anointing" but "The Rite of Anointing." Pope Paul VI, referring to the change in the prayers to be said while anointing the sick person explains: "We thought fit to modify the sacramental formula in such a way that, in view of the words of James, the effects of the sacrament might be more fully expressed." [15]

This accent on healing sets the sacrament within the great tradition of the Church which sees salvation in terms of healing. Paul Evdokimov has rightly remarked:

"For the Orient, salvation seen in the light of the Bible has nothing juridical about it. It is not the sentence of a tribunal. Jesus the Savior, according to the expression of Nicholas Cabasilas, is the 'divine healer,' the 'source of health,' he who said, 'It is not the healthy who need the doctor but the sick.' 'Your faith has saved you,' or 'Your faith has healed you' are synonyms for one and the same divine act which heals the soul and the body in their unity. In keeping with this therapeutic concept of salvation, the sacrament of confession is viewed as a 'medical clinic' and the Eucharist as the 'medicine of immortality.' " [16]

What emerges, therefore, as more important than simply reconciliation or the remission of sins is the integral restoration of the sick person by the action of the Holy Spirit. It is well to realize the complementary role of the sacraments and to recall that the Eucharist is given to us for "health in mind and body," and as the pledge of our future bodily resurrection. At the same time, the sacrament of reconciliation bears within it a healing power to which, in our theological treatises and pastoral teaching, sufficient attention has not been given.[17]

We might recall, too, that the sacrament of Orders is linked to healing. The ancient Church in Syria reminded a bishop on the day of his ordination that because he had been given the Holy Spirit for the forgiveness of sins, he had been constituted a "healer of the Church of God." In the Byzantine rite of today, there is mention of healing in the prayer for the ordination of both bishop and priest. Forgiveness and healing are alike associated with the action of the Holy Spirit. Indeed, a postcommunion prayer of the Roman rite during the former octave of Pentecost, says of the Holy Spirit, "He himself is the forgiveness of sins."

Prayer and Healing.

The changes in the sacrament of the sick should lead all of us to think afresh about our religious attitudes towards the sick; and to renew our faith in prayer for their healing.

The ministry of healing played too great a role in the life of Jesus for us to imagine that his work of restoring physical and moral health is not meant to be continued by his disciples. The Lord asks of us, as he did of his contemporaries, a faith that is expectant and confident, like that of the woman who reached out and touched the hem of his robe and was healed by a power that went forth from him.

We see in the early Church that "the many miracles and signs worked through the apostles made a deep impression on everyone" (Acts 2, 43). These cures were worked "in the name of Jesus and through faith in his name" (Acts 3, 16), and they were performed not only by the apostles but by other disciples. We read of Philip the deacon:

"The people united in welcoming the message Philip preached, either because they had heard of the miracles he worked or because they saw them for themselves. Unclean spirits came out with a loud cry from many who were possessed, and several paralytics and cripples were cured. As a result there was great rejoicing in that town" (Acts 8, 6–8).

We must renew within ourselves that faith in the power of the Lord to act in favour of the sick person. We should not be too hesitant in learning from examples of living faith that we see among our Protestant brothers. Then, too, we see within the heart of the Catholic Church, in those groups who are in touch with the Charismatic Renewal, a return to the practice of communal prayer for the sick. I begin to reflect on my own attitude when I visit the sick and find a group of Christians in the room, spontaneously praying for the one who is sick and laying their hands on him in a gesture which recalls that of Jesus in the Gospel and expresses their Christian union with the brother or sister who is suffering.

Often, we are afraid to believe who in fact we really are—that is to say, we are hesitant to believe in the Christ who lives and acts within us. We do not dare believe in prayer which can include miracles.

Those responsible for the teaching of the Church should, at every level, give us new and deeper instruction on the true meaning of prayer which always has its effect in accordance with the mind of God. We need to hear more of the true nature of God's fatherly love for us; the God of the living and not of the dead; the source of good and not of evil, who always wills the total well-being of his children. We need to hear more about the transforming and purifying power of suffering that is accepted in union with Jesus and which the Father always turns to the good of those whom he loves. Our prayer must embrace all the complexity of the world as it really is. There are sicknesses of every kind, seen and unseen, bodily, psychological, pathological, those which originate from some long forgotten traumatic experience. Our prayer must include all within us that has need of healing; we must open ourselves in all the dimensions of our human suffering, past as well as present, to the light of God's grace. We should remember that Jesus is the same yesterday and today, that he is Master of the past as well as of the present. If healings of a sudden spectacular nature are relatively rare, we must remember that slow, progressive healing is no less the work of God. Prayer is not in opposition to medical healing, but rather at its heart. It is common knowledge that in the world of medicine the attitude is no longer simply materialistic and positivist; on the contrary, it is increasingly conscious and respectful of all the factors that make up man.

In the light of a renewed Christian teaching on prayer and healing,[18] we can hope that all of us will take to heart, even outside a priestly and sacramental context, the words of St. James:

"If one of you is ill, he should send for the elders of the church, and they must anoint him with oil in the name of the Lord and pray over him. The prayer of faith will save the sick man and the Lord will raise him up again; and if he has committed any sins, he will be forgiven. So confess your sins to one another, and pray for one another, and this will cure you" (Jas. 5, 14–16).

Let us not forget that the Holy Spirit himself is that living and divine anointing in the power of which Jesus carried out his work. "God anointed Jesus of Nazareth with the Holy Spirit and with power, and because God was with him, he went about doing good and curing all who had fallen into the power of the devil" (Acts 10, 38).

PENTECOST IN LITURGY AND IN LIFE.

We could go through the whole ritual and meditate upon the role of the Holy Spirit as contained and expressed in the ritual of each sacrament, but these few remarks must suffice. We can appreciate without difficulty the truth that the Church is founded on the Eucharist and on Pentecost. Indeed Easter and Pentecost make up a single reality. In the light of their mutual interpenetration, we should look upon Pentecost as the culmination of the Paschal mystery and open ourselves to that action of the Holy Spirit upon which the liturgy of Pentecost meditates so magnificently.

The prayer which opens the Eucharistic celebration is of exceptional depth and beauty:

> "Lord, today, by the mystery of Pentecost
> you sanctify your Church among all peoples and nations.
> Pour out the gifts of the Holy Spirit
> over the whole world
> and continue in the hearts of believers
> that work of love which you began
> at the first preaching of the Gospel."

In the missal for English-speaking Canada, this prayer is also offered at the opening of the liturgy:

> "Father of light from whom every good gift comes,
> send your Spirit into our lives
> with the power of an irresistible wind,
> and by the flame of your wisdom
> open the horizon of our minds.
> Loosen our tongues to sing your praise
> in words beyond the power of speech,
> for without your Spirit it is not given to man
> to raise his voice in words of peace
> or announce the truth that Jesus is Lord." [19]

Tradition also contains among its treasures the sequence, "Come Holy Spirit," whose every word is a prayer in honor of the Holy Spirit radiant with the experience of the mystics and the saints.

Finally, going beyond the liturgy, but inspired by it, we must find again and pass on to the world, the fire of Pentecost: the light and the warmth of an authentic brotherly love.

To link the Eucharist and Pentecost is to proclaim that Christianity is a religion of love. A Christian is not only called to love his brethren with all his heart, but to love them with the heart of God. It is not enough that we love one another *for* the love of God, we must love one another *with* the love of God. There is a world of difference between philanthropy, excellent though it may be, and true Christian love which has its source in God himself. God awaits from us, as a sign of our Christian authenticity, that we love all men and the world in the power of that Love who is the Holy Spirit. The world, for its part, awaits from us Christians as a sign of credibility a love, the quality of which goes beyond the ordinary. When speaking of atheists, we should first acknowledge our own faults, as the Constitution *On the Church in the World* has done already and then ask ourselves: "Will not the fault be ours if atheists form a false idea of God, when we Christians have failed to reveal to them that God is Love?" On the other hand, when a Christian lives as Christ would have him live, he radiates a love which draws others to him.

Speaking of his entry into the Church, a convert said these striking words: "I believe the greatest truth is there, where there is the greatest love." The Church lives the two mysteries of the Eucharist and Pentecost; its renewal will depend upon the degree to which we Christians give witness to the mystery of a love that seems twofold, but in fact is indivisible. This is the challenge presented to us.

In drawing attention to the living reality of the Holy Spirit in the Church, the liturgical renewal brings us to a greater awareness of the role and place of religious experience itself. Indeed renewal means an awareness of the ever faithful, ever active presence of God among us. The Holy Spirit enables us to experience the immediacy of God in the heart of man and in history; this experience is essential to Christianity. The Christian religion does not put us into contact with God by means of some purely human mediation; rather, it is the unifying work of God himself. As Heribert Muehlen has expressed it: "Our relationship to the Holy Spirit is not one of a face to face: the Spirit is the immediacy of our face to face relationship with Christ and with the Father." [20]

We know the Father in the Son: "To have seen me is to have seen the Father" (Jn. 14, 9). And we know the Son by the Holy Spirit. But the Spirit is his own mediation. His presence is direct and immediate; a mysterious stirring, a whisper deep within us. This leads us to ask ourselves about the experiential aspect of the Christian life. We will consider this in the next chapter.

IV

The Holy Spirit and
the Experience of God

*The Spirit of truth, whom the world cannot
receive, because it neither sees him
nor knows him; you know him, for he dwells
with you, and will be in you.*
JOHN 14, 17

The presence of the Holy Spirit is not simply a doctrine of faith; it is perceived in the Church's tradition as a living experience that reveals itself in and through a variety of numerous and ever fresh manifestations. To have a context for this multiform experience, we should first ask ourselves about the possibility and the meaning of the manifestation of God in the world.

In his book *The Christian Experience*, Jean Mouroux writes: "The problem of the Christian experience necessarily arises in any philosophy of religion, or any theology. It is a major problem for the religious person, whose one wish is to form a relationship with God—to see him, touch him, feel him. In the hope of finding God, he gropes with his hands like a blind man (Acts 17, 27). Indeed the problem of the experience of God arises inevitably in any practice of religion or any religious thought. But it is felt without doubt more acutely when the conscience is a Christian one." [1]

Can God really enter our field of experience by some special act as distinct from that presence of his which is creative, extensive and immanent? Where will we meet God? Is he the conclusion of our syllogisms? Is he the keystone that supports the structure of our thought? Or is he a personal, warm, attentive presence at the heart of our life? Is he the God postulated by philosophy who gives an ultimate meaning to our world, or is he the living God, in the biblical sense, who touches our hearts?

Whatever may be the experience of the Spirit upon which we may wish to reflect, this basic question must be examined before we can discuss any specific experience. But let us admit it: it takes courage to abandon our cerebral pattern of thought and a manner of speech which is becoming every day more obscure, more closed in upon self, to begin to talk the simple, direct language of an experience that is lived.

I. YOUTH AND THE EXPERIENCE OF GOD.

Bishop G. Huyghe of Arras raises the objection often made against religious experience: "You dare to speak of a personal experience of God? Nonsense! You claim to help others to make this experience or even presume to share it with them? Is not this a temptation to escape the hardships of life, the exigencies of a real commitment and the arid loneliness of the apostolate?"

And he puts the question which is in the minds of many: "Is it not enough to speak to people *about* Jesus Christ? Then comes the answer: 'It's one thing to speak about

Jesus Christ, quite another and infinitely more important, to speak *to* Jesus Christ and to listen to his Spirit.' "

Bishop Huyghe goes on to say that, in the Bible, "to know" is an existential reality and "to know God" means to enter into a personal relationship with him:

"People often speak nowadays and with reason, about a new language of faith. Adults, theologians or not, make great efforts to fashion this difficult language. If they are trying to communicate a 'doctrine' even by carefully formulated concepts, they fail to make themselves understood.

"Young people will not come to faith through the teaching of dogmas, but by personal experience of God in Jesus Christ. Such an experience has to touch them at the level of concrete existence and should be formulated in their own words. . . .
"Faith today must be personalized: expressed, prayed and shared. It is an event, a meeting." [2]

This is how it was at the beginning. It was not the truth *about* Jesus but the truth *of* Jesus which was at the basis of conversion. Faith is born primarily of a personal meeting with the Lord. Teaching has an indispensable role, but existentially it has no priority.

The young have something to tell us on this subject, and they deserve our attention. Their total questioning, by its very radicalism, invites us to reflect. Certainly, the Gospel as proclaimed by a number of the young people—I am thinking, for instance, of the "Jesus Movement" or the "Jesus Freaks"—is not a complete Gospel; there are pages missing. The Jesus whom they preach is not the Jesus of a mature faith. Often the divine dimension is lacking; so is an understanding of the real meaning of redemptive salvation. Furthermore their reading of the Bible often accords with the fundamentalist pattern. Yet, despite these defects and ambiguities, young people are seeking in Jesus a reason for hope and a means of freeing themselves from the many forms of slavery in which we live today; they look for a way to breathe fresh air in the morally polluted climate of our time.

Robert Kennedy used to say that the tragedy of young people in America is that they have everything but the one thing which matters most: a reason for living.

Moreover, they are aware of this in a confused kind of way. But if they are to find in Jesus Christ this ultimate reason for living, then they must see in us a Gospel that is living. This is a grave hour for the Church. In the nineteenth century, we lost the working class; shall we now, in the twentieth century, lose the young?

II. EXPERIENTIAL AND EXPERIMENTAL.

The young are not alone in wanting to experience God. This longing is deep in the heart of every human being. Someone may object that this was so when St. Augustine wrote: "You have made us for yourself, O Lord, and our hearts cannot rest until they find rest in you." But it is not as simple as this now. Today, the secularization of the world, and the modern scientific turn of mind have eliminated God as an unnecessary hypothesis; there is no room for God in a scientifically controlled field of experience. For modern man "verity is verifiable." Where is there a place for God in our statistical analyses, or in a society that is at the mercy of computers?

Jean Mouroux expresses our contemporary climate admirably in these lines: "The contemporary consciousness, moreover, is such as to make this problem more urgent than ever. Today, experience is all-important, for we live in an age of experiences. The transformation of the material world, the control of life, the cynical grinding down of human material, the revolutionary artistic activity, the new efforts in all the realms of the spirit, violent, anarchic, perverted—all these things mean that we are plunged into a chaos of experiences. And when the modern man turns towards Christianity, the question he asks is, 'What worthwhile experience can you give me?' " [3]

In answering this challenge we must first bear in mind that the term "experience" can apply to many diverse realities. Philosophers distinguish between the words "experiential" and "experimental." The first designates a living perception and knowledge of the concrete, not to be confused with the experiments made in our laboratories.[4] The experience of God, of which we are speaking, obviously pertains to the first term, though this knowledge does not contradict knowledge gained through experimentation; it simply transcends it, indeed it is on "another wave length."

The constant temptation of the man of science is to reduce what is real to what he can attain to by his own exclusive methods, and to forget that certain realities are not attainable by means of the scalpel or the telescope. True scientists however, are generally modest in this respect; they realize their limitations. Many have attested that their faith was sustained by a personal experience of God, and that, as faith grew, God's action became more real to them in their daily existence.

There is no need to present here testimonials in support of this. Let us rather point to a convergence. For these men, as for ourselves, faith is normally received and lived before it is formulated, and it takes root and becomes aware of itself as the result of an experience of God.

To penetrate the secrets of nature requires powerful and precise instruments. To penetrate the secrets of the hidden presence of God in ourselves and in human history, we need a power that goes beyond our own resources. To search out the realm of the invisible we need a light whose rays are more delicate and piercing than infra-red. This power, this light, is the Holy Spirit who "alone explores the depths of God."

The special mission of the Spirit is to reveal not himself, but Jesus, the unique Son of God. Within each Christian heart, the Spirit is faithful to this mission: he accompanies us step by step, shedding on our path, as we advance in faith, a light from within. It is normal, too, that our apprehension, so to speak, of the way God works is an experience unlike any other. It takes place within the context of faith; of itself, without faith, it would not be recognizable as an experience of God. "No one can say 'Jesus is Lord' unless it be granted to him by the Holy Spirit" (1 Cor. 12, 3).

It is natural then, that the manifestation of God's intimate, personal, and direct presence should take place within the life of the Church and in the personal life of each Christian.

III. FAITH AND EXPERIENCE

Basically, the problem is that of harmonizing what seem to be opposites. How can we reconcile an experiential manifestation of God with faith, which by definition believes without seeing, relying solely on the word of God? Is it possible to abandon oneself to God, to leap into the water and at the same time feel the ground firm under one's feet?

CONTRADICTION?

Are not faith and experience contradictory? Is it possible to reconcile the dark night of faith with the brilliance of the stars?

At first sight, it would seem that faith and experience are mutually exclusive. Faith, by definition, is an adherence to God who reveals himself and who summons us to accept his word as the ultimate truth of life, because of his own intrinsic credibility and in the very mystery which envelops him. Can one rend the veil of the temple, and yet not violate its sacredness?

Does not Scripture tell us: "The upright man finds life through faith" (see Rom. 1, 17 etc.)? And has not Jesus proclaimed: "Happy are those who have not seen but have believed" (Jn. 20, 29)? Then, too, the whole spiritual tradition of the Church teaches us not to confuse true faith with whatever perception of it we may possess. To believe with real faith is one thing, to experience emotion while believing is another. "I believe, help my unbelief" (Mk. 9, 24). This cry of a father asking that his son be healed is a cry of hesitant faith which is not infrequent. We carry these treasures in fragile vessels. Would it not undermine faith if we were to wish, not to substitute experience for faith—something no one wants to do—but to give it some exterior support under the pretext of making it firmer?

SUBJECTIVISM?

But even if faith and experience can be harmonized, a question remains: is this not endangering the objectivity of our faith, the needed acceptance of doctrinal truths revealed by God and guaranteed by the hierarchical Church, in favour of our subjectivity?

As to this last point, let us rid ourselves immediately of any misunderstanding. We must not forget that faith is basically an adherence, not to a set of propositions, but to God who reveals himself to us. Faith is a living encounter with a living God; it is formulated in the Church within the context of experience. Doctrine is the expression or common definition of the experience of God, as lived by the apostles and the Christian community and then passed on to us. In his first letter, St. John testifies to what he and the other disciples witnessed day by day.

"Something which has existed since the beginning, that we have heard, and we have seen with our own eyes; that we have watched and touched with our hands: the Word, who is life—this is our subject. That life was made visible: we saw it and we are giving our testimony, telling you of the eternal life which was with the Father and has been made visible to us" (1 Jn. 1, 1–2).

Experiencing Christ comes of necessity before the definition of that experience. St. Thomas Aquinas, a theologian whom no one would suspect of anti-intellectualism, teaches that the object of faith is not found in doctrinal propositions concerning God, but in God himself known and loved in a personal relationship.[5]

Doctrine is important for many reasons. For one thing it serves as an objective criterion in the Christian community by which we may judge the authenticity of each subjective experience; this latter must not contradict the former. But the doctrinal teaching which enunciates truths regarding Christ is first of all rooted in the experience of meeting him. The same applies to truths regarding the Holy Spirit. The early Christians first of all lived an experience of the Holy Spirit—and with what joy! The dogma of the Holy Spirit was defined only three centuries later. For these Christians, to receive the Spirit and to experience the Spirit were one and the same thing.

EXAGGERATIONS.

The experiential dimension of Christianity, to which the New Testament bears witness, was pushed to extremes in certain theories concerning sanctification. The Jansenists sought to experience predestination, the Quietists a total spiritual passivity, while the Modernists wished to situate the essence of Christianity in a subjective experience of life rather than in the truths set out in the Creed. Within Protestantism, too, Schleiermacher extolled a religion of romantic sentiment, and William James made of religious experience a sort of self-sufficient interior authority.

Fear of excess explains the insistence of the *Magisterium* on the objective aspect of religion in the matter of doctrine and the sacraments. But the fear of abuse must not minimize the meaning and the role of religious experience at the heart of authentic Christianity. All the more so in that religion addresses itself to the whole man who is neither pure spirit nor a disembodied soul, but a being who is both matter and spirit, who sees, feels, reflects and acts.

This integration of experience in the religious life of the Christian community is an authentic continuation that comes down to us from the Old Testament. For the Israelites, to know God was to experience him. In the biblical view of man, there is only one approach to knowledge, and that passes through experience. This principle applies equally to the knowledge of God. The Jews only knew God in and through their concrete historical experience. They had nothing equivalent to our abstract, metaphysical speculation about his nature and his attributes. They knew Yahweh because they had experienced his saving action. Was it not he who had led them out of the land of Egypt? Jewish prayer often alludes to this experience; and the history of Israel, within which God manifested himself, was at one with their prayer:

"Listen to his Law my people,
pay attention to what I say;
I am going to speak to you in parables
and expound the mysteries of our past.
What we have heard and known for ourselves,
and what our ancestors have told us,
must not be withheld from their descendants,
but be handed on by us to the next generation" (Ps. 78, 1–4).

BIBLICAL LANGUAGE.

In the biblical conception of truth, the bond linking

truth and experience is strongly accented. Walter Kasper, in considering certain aspects of Hebrew thought, comments: "The Hebrew does not occupy himself much with what is, but with what happens and with what he experiences in the concrete. . . . Things and people are to be relied upon and true if they fulfill the expectations that one had of them and if they justify the confidence that one cherished in their regard . . . Thus truth always transpires and is manifested in time. . . . That which possesses duration, consistence, and future is true."

This does not make all truth relative nor does it deprive metaphysics of its rights. But these observations set truth within perspective of the Bible.

In the Old Testament, the emphasis was on the active presence of God outside man; in the New Testament this same presence is primarily seen as being within. It is the penetrating action of God's love in the soul which, in faith, reveals the divine presence: "Everybody who believes in the Son of God has this testimony within him" (1 Jn. 5, 10). This enables us to understand better the words of Jesus when he tells us: "He who does what is true comes out into the light" (Jn. 3, 21). Faith and experience must mutually evoke one another and we should accept that they are of necessity complementary.[6]

What we have said applies to authentic religious experience. But that does not mean, alas, that there are no counterfeits. The Church knows too well and is justifiably on guard against a subjectivism which periodically appears as a threat to the faith.

ILLUMINISM.

The history of religious illuminism is long, both within the Catholic Church and outside. Already in the second century, Montanism—the best known exponent of which was Tertullian—laid claims to new revelations and announced the end of the world in the ecstatic language associated with visionaries.

In the middle ages, Joachim of Flora announced the beginning of the third age of the world, that of the Holy Spirit. Exalting to excess the role of the Holy Spirit, he presented the age of the Spirit as succeeding that of the Father (the Old Testament) and that of the Son (the New Testament). The Church had to reject this break in continuity and this view of these successive stages in the history of salvation.

Throughout history a certain number of religious orders have had to force their way forward in the Church in the midst of pseudo-mystic movements with which they were at first confused. Part of the difficulties they underwent came from this confusion. Every century has had its share of pseudo-mystic excesses, either quietist or apocalyptic.

The Protestant Churches have also regularly been confronted, along with genuine currents of revival, with false movements based on a fundamentalist biblical interpretation or on experiences that were either on the fringe or openly incompatible with their traditions. A book such as Ronald Knox's *Enthusiasm* will help one not to forget the need for critical evaluation in such matters.[7]

These periodic excesses explain the prudence of the hierarchy. A negative reaction is more than understandable; however, the last word belongs by right to an enlightened faith. The discernment of spirits is a charism to be used with special wisdom in accordance with the counsel of St. Paul when speaking of manifestations of the Spirit: "Do not stifle inspiration and do not despise prophetic utterance, but bring them all to the test and then keep what is good in them and avoid the bad of whatever kind" (1 Thess. 5, 19–20).

EXPERIENCE AND THE CHRISTIAN LIFE.

Despite the ever present possibility of deviations, Jesus did not exclude religious experience from the Christian life.

We are not speaking here of mystical experience, a special type of experience which theologians discuss as to whether or not it is a normal goal in a mature Christian life. We are concerned with the ordinary experience of God. Jesus did not present aridity as the normal condition of the Christian life. The way of a St. John of the Cross or a St. Teresa of Avila whom God purified in mystic depths by having them pass through the night of the senses and the spirit is one thing; the usual way by which the ordinary Christian "walks with God" is another.

The Gospel is profoundly human; Jesus knows the heart of man. At his first meeting with Nathanael, the Master remarked that he had seen him under the fig tree. Nathanael was astounded at this special attention, whereon Jesus promised him that he would see yet greater things. Thus, evidently, for Jesus, the night of faith is not pitch dark and devoid of stars. We should take seriously those sayings of his scattered throughout the Gospels, in which he promised "a peace the world cannot give" (Jn. 14, 27), and a joy that "no one shall take from you" (Jn. 16, 22).

The Lord did not promise his followers that they would be without suffering. On the contrary, he repeatedly stressed the necessity of carrying the cross in his wake and he prepared them for it. But he promised that, at the same time, he would give them peace and joy even in the midst of suffering, and it is this which makes all the difference. Herein is the serenity to which his disciples bear witness: their personal experience had taught them that his "yoke is easy and his burden light." They know also the truth of his promise: "Anyone who loves me will be loved by my

Father, and I shall love him and reveal myself to him" (Jn. 14, 21).

May I say in passing that I do not need a series of manifestations of God to verify these promises. One single experience, lived to the full, is enough to confirm the reality of the divine presence, just as one ray of sunlight enables me to realize the splendor of the sun. Moreover to enjoy the sun's warmth, it is not necessary to be able to define solar energy.

The entire life of the early Church bears witness to the fulfillment of the Lord's promises. Besides the Acts of the Apostles, where the manifestations of God often stand out dramatically because of their charismatic nature, the rest of the New Testament illustrates in simple day-to-day incidents that the Lord does not fail to keep his promises.

Paul speaks often of the fruits of the Spirit. These fruits, signs of his authentic presence, can be felt, touched, savored. They are, St. Paul tells the Galatians, ". . . love, joy, peace, patience, kindness, goodness, trustfulness, gentleness and self-control" (Gal. 5, 22–23). Such are the signs, the proofs, of authentic Christianity. There is no doubt whatsoever that the Spirit bestows such fruits on all who are truly open to receive him, whether they know him by name or not. "Your love shines on us like the sun at midday," one of our liturgical texts says. Still, in a Christian who is faithful to the Spirit, this love, joy and peace have a unique quality, a certain intensity, revealing to those who have eyes to see a hidden presence . . . like the sanctuary lamp, reminding us of the Presence in the tabernacle.

In accordance with the logic of the Gospel, the liturgy teaches us to pray to the Lord for the grace to love truly what he commands. The Lord knows our need of peace and interior joy so as to walk better at his side.

Those of us who belong to northern European cultures still bear the marks of Jansenism; its traces have not been completely eliminated. Recently, when I was attending a session of the Second National Conference on the Holy Spirit organized by the Charismatic Communion of Presbyterian Ministers in the United States, I heard the president of the Congress say, to the amusement of all: "God told us we were his *chosen*, not his *frozen* people."

The Church in her liturgy does not hesitate to ask for perceptible manifestations of God. For centuries we have been saying quite naturally: "O God, who by the light of the Holy Spirit didst instruct the hearts of the faithful, grant, we beseech Thee, that by the same Holy Spirit, we may be always truly wise and ever rejoice in his consolations." We need only recall the prayers and hymns that tradition has given to us, the hymns *Veni, Sancti Spiritus* or *Jesu dulcis memoria*, the prayers of St. Bernard or St. Bonaventure and so many others, to realize with what intensity the Church has always prayed for the outpouring of the Spirit's gifts, the gift of tears among them.

These brief reflections show that we are without doubt true to the full traditional spirituality of the Church.

IV. ENCOUNTERS WITH GOD.

As some people see it, this talk about "experiencing God" is simply an escape from the world; to concentrate on "God alone" is to cut oneself off from our fellowmen, their sufferings and problems. This is not so if the experience of God is genuine. Indeed, such a dichotomy would be the negation of any authentic experience.

One of the great mystics of this century, a man whose life on Mt. Athos was already an exceptional vocation to prayer and an apparent "denial of the world," described as follows the monastic ideal of "pure prayer": "Sometimes, the Holy Spirit draws a man so completely to Himself that he forgets all created things and gives himself entirely to contemplation of God. But when the soul remembers the world again, filled with the love of God, she feels compassion for all and prays for the whole world. In thus praying, the soul may again forget the world and repose in God alone, only to return once more to her prayer for all mankind." [8]

Openness to God is synonymous with openness to the world of men which God has created, loved and sanctified. To love God is to enter into the mystery of God whereby he so loved us that he gave his only begotten Son who, in his turn, left us his commandment that we love one another.

Let us now consider that authentic experience of God which should be a normal reality in the life of every Christian.

EXPERIENCE, ORDINARY AND EXTRAORDINARY.

We might be tempted to distinguish two kinds of experience: one ordinary, the other extraordinary. Such a distinction is false. It is based on our way of judging, in so far as the meeting with God seemed, or did not seem, in our view, to be unexpected, unusual or unique. But this is foreign to God's way of judging.

For God there is no line of demarcation between "ordinary" and "extraordinary." He crosses with ease the dotted line that marks our frontiers. In God the extraordinary is ordinary.

God does not love us with ordinary love, making some exceptions from time to time. No, the *extraordinary* love of God is part of his very being: our God is a God who is wonderful, even prodigal, in his love for men. The most astonishing proofs of his love—the Incarnation, the Eucharist, the Cross—all go beyond anything we would expect or imagine. Scripture tells us quite simply: "God so loved the world that he gave his only Son" (Jn. 3, 16). This unbelievable gesture of love wells up from the depths of his heart, and overflows on mankind.

As we look upon it, such love takes our breath away. It goes beyond anything we could dare imagine and it makes us realize that God loves us to the point of miracle. Jesus said: "Truly, truly, I say to you, he who believes in me will also do the works I do, and greater works than I do, because I go to the Father" (Jn. 14, 12). Such a promise should not surprise us: for God, the supernatural is natural; he is marvelous by his very nature. Our most condensed *credo* is contained in the words: "We ourselves have known and put our faith in the love God has for us" (1 Jn. 4, 16). This is why we dare believe in the power of prayer, because we have before our eyes the picture of Jesus, saying to his Father, even before he put his prayer into words: "Father, I thank you for hearing my prayer. I know indeed that you always hear me . . ." (Jn. 11, 41–42). This "always" is an integral part of our faith, even when our reason is shrouded in darkness.

We have to learn to discover this extraordinary love of God, hidden in a happening which is apparently, perfectly ordinary, completely accidental: "If you believe, you will see the glory of God" (Jn. 11, 40).

There are times when God pierces the obscurity of faith like a flash of lightning in the pitch darkness of the night. We may not always be able to put these experiences into words. Indeed they are well-nigh impossible to communicate: yet they are very real, and lives are transformed by them. Bergson once said: "God created the world and overturns it to make saints." And this action of God, whether hidden or apparent, continues all through the history of the Church.

It overpowered Mary at the Annunciation, when she suddenly realized she was blessed and chosen among all women.

It was there, on Easter morn, under the guise of a gardener, calling her by name, Mary of Magdala.

It filled with burning fire the hearts of the discouraged disciples on the way to Emmaus.

It unhorsed Paul and struck him blind on the road to Damascus.

It whispered to Augustine: "Take up and read," and thus changed his life.

It so illumined a verse of Scripture—as when a sudden ray of sunshine lights up and brings out all the beauty of a stained-glass window—that a Francis of Assisi took literally the words: "If you would be perfect, go and sell all you have and give it to the poor . . . then come, follow me" (Mt. 19, 21).

It takes a thousand forms and changes a thousand times for each of us.

It is hidden in the gentle light or the glowing blaze, revealing to us our vocation or the mission entrusted to us.

It is hidden in the unexpected encounter with a friend at a crossroad saying, as did Ananias to Paul, the decisive word. A meeting no one could have foreseen but which confirms what a spiritual writer was not afraid to say: "If a man needs another to tell him 'the necessary word' God will bring that man to him from the ends of the earth."

It pursues its aim under cover of what we call 'haphazard events,' which are nothing other than God himself at work, directing secondary courses and what we call coincidences and chance happenings: all instruments of a love that is all-pervading, resourceful and steadfast beyond belief.

God writes extraordinary novels for those of us who are ready "to play his game," willing to be open to the unexpected, on the alert to hear the whispers of grace and the promptings of the Spirit.

This experience of God, which is within the scope of every Christian, does not remove suffering nor quell the powers of evil—these are part of our earthly condition. The world is like a Rembrandt painting, a play of light and darkness. God comes to us, not as the Omnipotent One, crushing our human freedom, but as a love, infinitely vulnerable in search of a free response. Claudel said: "Jesus did not come to explain suffering nor to take it away: he came to fill it with his presence." Words with a depth of meaning. They do not, it is true, clarify the mystery of iniquity and evil. Nevertheless, they temper its darkness with the light of Golgotha. For there God showed that he is "on our side" in our conflict with sin and suffering. These he has taken upon himself to make of them new elements of our redemption.

The discovery that God is at the very heart of suffering is for many of the sick, a living experience in the face of which we can only marvel. Despite their pain, they smile, and their serenity sheds light on the lives of the rest of us. God is there in a special way, identifying himself with this suffering, in a way that only Gethsemane can explain. "*Ogni dolore è Lui,*" "Every suffering is He," says Chiara Lubich, who founded the Focolare movement.

A PERSONAL APPROACH.

For my own part, as the years go by, I become increasingly aware of God's wonderfully active presence in my life, and of my poor correspondence to his many graces. The revelation of his unfailing concern, which finds no detail too small, awakes within me a hymn of joyful praise whose refrain could be from one of our glorious antiphons at Chrismastide: "O Wisdom, you reach from beginning to end, ordering all things with strength and sweetness."

This thanksgiving easily takes the form of a litany in which I enumerate a name, a memory, a date, a coincidence. I say to God "thank you" for advice given in a moment of crisis, a book read casually which had a message for me, a telephone call, a letter, a suffering, an encouragement. And, permeating and binding all these, is my thanks to him for a joy and a peace that no one can take from me because they are beyond the reach of man.

This is like saying the rosary: the beads slipping through my fingers, one mystery succeeding another: joyful, sorrowful and glorious. Each bead recalls some attention shown me by God, a sign, a meeting. I end with a "Glory be to the Father," a thanksgiving for the love of God which has been waiting for me at every turn of my life, at every detour on the road.

When I think of God's love in wait, I recall the poem that is for me the most beautiful of all: Francis Thompson's "The Hound of Heaven." Each person can interpret the poem differently in the light of his own life. But the God who is "on the watch" to pursue us with his love, like a "heavenly hound," is the same for all. His concern for us, multiplying itself to infinity, is there in its entirety for each one of us; it is the thread which weaves every human life into a single whole.

Every Christian should reflect upon his life in the light of faith—this will give him the key to its meaning—and entrusting himself to God, allow God to flood his entire being. He should be ready to share his secret with the world and proclaim aloud his joy.

This awareness of God, present, familiar, close to us, becomes more perceptive and delicate as we learn to recognize the many signs of God, who shows his attentive presence and his oneness with us, by a look, a gesture, as would a friend. God speaks a language particular to each person; it is spoken softly, yet audibly. Each of us must learn God's alphabet, to spell with it, read with it, recognize and understand it.

Sometimes we decipher the message badly: we think that this God who appears before us and beckons to us, is some sort of phantom. He has to say to us as he said to his disciples: "It is I, do not be afraid" (Jn. 6, 20).

I like to compare our approach to God in faith to that of a traveler who, as he makes his way on a winter night, arrives by some detour at a lonely cottage, ablaze with lights shining through the windows. As he looks through the windows, he sees a fire with logs burning and crackling and sparks flying. He can imagine the warmth by the fireplace, but he cannot feel it as long as he stays outside, an onlooker, in the cold and wind. This is an image of the Christian who, in the darkness of faith, sees the light and warmth that is God.

He can say with the psalmist: "The night is my light and my joy" (Ps. 139, 11). Still, though he may catch sight of the firelight and imagine its warmth, it has not yet penetrated to the very marrow of his bones. He has yet to go inside, not because he is worthy, but because God invites him: a God who gently presses the invitation, and longs to be one with him. For that to happen, the traveler must knock at the door—that is what he has to do. Jesus told us to knock. He did not say how many times. We have to be sure to knock and knock again. But above all, each one of us must realize that he is expected at the fireside, that he is a son, that this is his home, that he can give no greater joy to God than by accepting his invitation.

To stay on the threshold on the plea of humility would be to misjudge God's heart. He invites all of us to experience, even here below, the warmth of his love; he has made us just for that.

Once he is inside, everything is different for the traveler. The bright flames on the hearth leap up to greet him, the heat begins to envelop, to penetrate him, his face lights up in the glow, he reaches out his two hands, and his numb limbs begin to lose their numbness. A sort of osmosis begins; the brightness of the flames penetrates his very being. This is an image of the experience of God, as felt by one who lets himself be invaded by God, who opens his whole being, conscious and subconscious, to the radiance of his presence. A new life takes over. St. Paul's cry becomes, once more, a reality: "It is no longer I who live, it is Christ who lives in me" (Gal. 2, 20).

We are not alone any more, we know we are guided by the Holy Spirit; our life unfolds in response to him. As we dispossess ourselves, our being is possessed by God. The void is filled.

God himself, who is all welcome, light and warmth, transforms our existence, bestowing on us something of his radiance. Those who allow themselves to be possessed by God, resemble the log that little by little becomes white-hot. Their life, nourished by the fire of the Holy Spirit, becomes fire in its turn. Is not this the fire of which Jesus spoke when he said: "I have come to bring fire to the earth . . ." (Lk. 12, 49)? This is what it means to experience the Holy Spirit who alone can renew the face of the earth!

The Holy Spirit and a Contemporary Religious Experience

Since the Spirit is our life,
let us be directed by the Spirit.
GALATIANS 5, 25

As Edward Schweizer remarked, long before the Spirit was a theme of doctrine, he was a fact in the experience of the community.[1]

This spiritual experience has never ceased in the history of the Church and it is at the heart of everything which bears the seal of God in the Church today. The fact, however, that we recognize this universal presence of the Spirit should not prevent us from discerning, analyzing, and reflecting upon a special and privileged presence where he manifests himself in a particular way. It is in this attitude of openess to what the Spirit does in his sovereign freedom, that I wish to call attention to the importance of a particular force of renewal in the Church today: the Charismatic Renewal or Renewal in the Spirit. I will first trace briefly its beginnings and listen to some personal witnesses; I will then attempt to analyze its meaning within the Church of today.

I. THE ORIGINS OF THE CHARISMATIC RENEWAL.

THE BIRTH OF THE CATHOLIC CHARISMATIC RENEWAL.

The beginnings of this renewal in the Catholic Church have been told in detail by Kevin and Dorothy Ranaghan in their book, *Catholic Pentecostals*[2], in which they describe, at first hand, how what is now called the Charismatic Renewal, originated. Another valuable testimony can be found in a work by Father Edward O'Connor, professor of theology at the University of Notre Dame who, in addition to recounting the events that marked the initial stirrings of the Spirit in 1967, also attempts a theological analysis in the light of the tradition of the Church. His book, *The Pentecostal Movement in the Catholic Church*[3], is like that of the Ranaghans a basic work on the subject of Charismatic Renewal. From then on studies and articles in many languages have appeared one after another. Let us begin with a brief account of the facts.

This Renewal first came into being in the Catholic Church among students in Duquesne University, Pittsburgh, Pennsylvania, during the year 1967. At a time of social and religious crises throughout their own country and the world at large, some of these young people, realizing the impossibility of finding a human solution, met for a weekend of prayer and fasting to ask the grace of the Holy Spirit[4].

Who were they? For the most part, members of the University already actively engaged in movements concerned with the liturgy, ecumenism, the struggle for civil rights, and efforts in support of world peace. The Ranaghans write of them: "In spite of all this they felt there was something lacking in their individual Christian lives. They couldn't quite put their finger on it but somehow there was an emptiness, a lack of dynamism, a sapping of strength in their lives of prayer and action. It was as if their lives as Christians were too much their own creation, as if they were moving forward under their own power and of their own will. It seemed to them that the Christian life wasn't meant to be a purely human achievement." [5]

These young people were Christians for whom the growing pains of the Church were a personal, deep and daily experience. Such was the background.

That weekend, for those who attended, proved to be, in the true sense of the word a new Pentecost. Nor had they gone to it unprepared. Many had read David Wilkerson's *The Cross and the Switchblade*.[6] This small book, which has sold in many thousands, recounts the personal story of a minister who, with faith in the Holy Spirit and under his guidance, transformed spiritually some of the toughest gang members of New York's slums, healing many who were addicted to drugs and helping many others as they got out of prison.

They had also read together St. Paul and the Acts of the Apostles and some of them had recited, every day for a year, the Sequence from the Octave of Pentecost, "Come, Holy Spirit." They kept in their heart that yearning for the new Pentecost for which John XXIII had prayed on the eve of the Second Vatican Council. All these factors had gone into the preparation for that weekend in February 1967, when these young people went on retreat together, to ask the Holy Spirit to come and renew the face of the Church and of the whole earth.

The Spirit's response to them was an experience, over again, of what happened when the first disciples of the Lord were together in the upper-room in Jerusalem. An amazing spiritual transformation took place in them. They spoke of a new awareness of the love of God such as they had not experienced before; of a desire to pray and glorify God; of an insatiable thirst for Scripture. Moreover they felt power within them to bear witness to the risen Jesus. They talked of a "baptism in the Holy Spirit" and of charisms given to them similar to those of which we read in the early Church. They did not consider this "baptism in the Holy Spirit" as in any way a replacement of the sacraments of baptism and confirmation. The key is to be found in the words of one of them: "It seemed, rather, a kind of adult re-affirmation and renewal of these sacraments, an opening of ourselves to all their sacramental graces".[7] In Chapter 7 we will return to this question, which we consider fundamental: this reaffirmation, at a mature age, of the sacraments of initiation.

The rest of the story is simple. These young people who had just experienced the marvels of the Lord had friends in other universities with whom, naturally, they shared what had happened. And so the universities of South Bend, Indiana, Ann Arbor, Michigan, Loyola, New Orleans and Los Angeles, began to experience the same enthusiasm and the same phenomena, the same outpouring of graces.

I have myself met many persons at these different universities who witnessed at first-hand what took place, and many of them have become my friends. Their witness makes a deep impression on me and their credibility seems beyond question.

Soon, "prayer groups" began to spring up not only on university campuses but also in parishes, monasteries and convents, first in the United States and then in the five continents. The first national conference, held in 1967, was attended by about one hundred people. In June 1973, I took part in the International Conference, held at South Bend, Indiana, on the campus of Notre Dame University, and attended by approximately twenty-two thousand people who came from thirty-five different countries and included about six hundred priests and some ten bishops. In 1974 the conference numbered over thirty thousand people with a comparable increase in the number of priests and bishops.

As the small prayer groups began to grow, some of them became weekly gatherings of hundreds of people. Sometimes these meetings are held within the context of a Eucharistic celebration, sometimes not.

Communities, more stable, more committed, called "households" sprang up, and these became the stable element in the prayer groups, especially in those more particularly engaged in social activity.

"Houses of prayer" have been founded which, in the context of schools of spirituality, are open to all. Their aim is to initiate as many people as possible into the Christian life as it has come recently to be experienced in this new light.

Another characteristic of the Renewal, where prayer groups are sufficiently mature, has been the creation of different types of communal living. I would mention as particularly remarkable the "Word of God" community in the university town of Ann Arbor, Michigan. There the experience in communal living involves some one thousand adherents to the Charismatic Renewal, of whom only ten percent are over thirty years of age. The majority of these live in "households" of ten or fifteen persons; their manner of living as a community and sharing what they possess takes various forms and is flexible. At the basis of this life in common is a serious and clear commitment to the other members of the household and the acceptance of a discipline decided upon by general consent. The goal of all concerned is to help one another to live a life true to the spirit of the Gospel and to give witness of this in the world.

Ann Arbor is also the center which publishes *New Covenant*, a monthly periodical at the service of Charismatic groups throughout the world. Its editor, Ralph Martin, is a young married man who is particularly qualified for his role. His book on prayer, *Hungry for God, Practical Helps in Personal Prayer*, which is soon to be published, will help readers to appreciate better the spiritual depth of this renewal.

II. WITNESSES.

The initial experience of these young university people quickly spread beyond their own milieu. People from all walks of life began to witness to a similar experience: manual workers, ex-prisoners, university professors, married couples, contemplative and active religious.

A remarkable thing has happened: without any mutual contact, it seems that the Spirit has initiated, in various parts of the world, experiences which, if not identical, are at least comparable. It is too soon to study all these testimonies and group them in categories. I will confine myself to mention a book recently published by Father George Kosicki, C.S.B., former professor of bio-chemistry at Windsor University, under the title, *The Lord is My Shepherd; the Witness of Priests*.[8] There is also the study by Father John Haughey, S.J., Associate editor of the magazine *America*. He published in one of the issues of *Studies in the Spirituality of the Jesuits*[9] the findings of forty members of the Society of Jesus who have personally experienced Charismatic Renewal in their own lives. As I looked through these pages, so moving in their sincerity, I noticed that there was a strong converging movement— the same words kept coming up as a leitmotiv—and at the same time the action of the Spirit was nuanced and differentiated according to each individual's personality.

Here we find men of more diverse and extensive experience, all of them followers of St. Ignatius, and all of them amazed to discover, with new eyes, the image of their founder and his own initial charism. So true is it that authentic charisms attract one another and meet in their common source: the Holy Spirit.

Father Haughey begins by remarking with a touch of humor that if the Jesuits all over the world, are divided in their views on practically every subject, they all agree to see St. Ignatius as a charismatic personality.

After pointing out that Ignatius' guidance in the area of discernment of spirits has been of immense importance in fostering authentic charisms, he goes on to add that the term "charismatic" cannot be used to define a closed sect any more than the term "Society of Jesus" means to exclude others from enjoying the company of the Master.

A questionnaire was put to forty Jesuits who had been involved in the Charismatic Renewal. It asked: "What has been the effect on you and on your vocation as a Jesuit of: (1) the baptism (in the Holy Spirit); (2) the gifts; (3) Charismatic prayer groups?" This was followed by a series of more general questions touching on how they had been personally affected by the Charismatic Renewal.

The answers fall under certain headings. I note first of all, the impressive unanimity in favor of the renewal. I will quote some typical responses.

In speaking of the "baptism in the Holy Spirit"—I will discuss later why it would be better to avoid this term—the majority recognized that this "spiritual experience" had touched them profoundly. An elderly priest wrote: "For a few weeks I was overwhelmed with consolations: an awareness of the presence of God; spontaneous tears and also laughter; a hunger, too, to be purified and a desire to read Scripture and pray for hours at a time with joy."

Another described his experience as feeling filled with a

new power. He stood up and with no preparation spoke for an hour and felt touched with a new power with texts from the Scriptures, words and examples came to him with a spontaneity that amazed him. He ended saying: "I had earlier written a book, but now the words and ideas it contained became a living reality."

Briefly, what seems to be common to all is an experience of a presence and of a power coming from the Holy Spirit. There is also a change in the climate of prayer: "My prayer is less intellectual now, simpler, more from the heart and much more filled with praise." Several gave testimony to the spiritual fruits they experienced by praying in tongues. Others spoke of a change which made them more deeply and constantly aware of the presence of God in their apostolic activity, and they felt their preaching vivified from within by the Holy Spirit. They spoke of the spiritual support they found in prayer groups, and of a new boldness in sharing with their brothers deeper, inner experiences, despite the conventional inhibitions that prevail among religious. Others mentioned, too, a change in their attitude toward the sacrament of penance which they now saw as a sacrament of spiritual healing. In general, these men testified that this experience had strengthened them in their Jesuit vocation, and sometimes even in their priesthood, and that it had led them to see in a new light . . . the exercises of St. Ignatius!

These are some of the reactions that can be gleaned from Father Haughey's profound and profitable study. I would like to add, for my part, that many priests, religious, and lay people, both men and women, have told me of similar spiritual experiences, often in the same terms as those of these forty Jesuits. Such testimonies are not only from America; I have heard their like in various countries of the world: every day their number increases from continent to continent. This should be more than enough to convince us of the necessity of studying this experience at close quarters.

III. ATTEMPT TO ANALYZE A SPIRITUAL EXPERIENCE.

Testimony to an experience is one thing, analysis of that experience is another. The credibility of those who testify obliges me to pay attention, but it does not provide the theological interpretation to be given to what they have lived and are still living. Specialists have here a relatively new field to explore. Thanks be to God there are theologians and exegetes in our universities who are reflecting on this experience, not as observers from without but as interpreters from within. For example, Herbert Muehlen, professor of theology at the University of Paderborn and a recognized specialist in the field of pneumatology, will soon be publishing a book on this subject. Every day new theological studies are being published. It is no longer totally fallow ground, yet there still remain riches in the soil and in the sub-soil to be exploited.

Here we wish to limit ourselves to an analysis of the initial religious experience of conversion and the outpouring of the Spirit: what is currently called "baptism in the Spirit." What should we understand by this phrase?

1. THE MEANING OF "BAPTISM IN THE SPIRIT."

On the level of actual experience, we can and indeed must admire classical Pentecostals for their faith in the action of the Holy Spirit. However, as everyone knows, as Catholics we cannot follow them on a doctrinal and exegetical level in their interpretation of "baptism in the Spirit" nor in the matter of speaking in tongues, which they regard as the sign that authenticates this baptism. For us, as well as for the majority of Christian Churches, there is not a duality of baptisms, one in water and one in the Spirit. We believe there is but one baptism. Baptism in the Holy Spirit is not a sort of super-baptism, or a supplement to sacramental baptism which would then become the pivot of the Christian life.[10]

With St. Paul we believe that in his gratuitous goodness "God saved us through the water of rebirth and the renewing power of the Holy Spirit. For he sent down the Spirit upon us plentifully through Jesus Christ our Saviour, so that, justified by his grace, we might in hope become heirs to eternal life" (Tit. 3, 5–7).

Our one and only baptism is at the same time both paschal and pentecostal. To avoid from now on all ambiguity it would be better not to speak of "baptism in the Spirit" but to look for another expression.

2. THE EXPERIENCE OF THE SPIRIT AND OF CHARISMS.

How then can we define and assess more clearly and precisely this initial experience of the Holy Spirit? It is a delicate task to try to put in words the action of the Holy Spirit which, of necessity, eludes our categories! Moreover we are faced with the difficulty of speaking about a new outpouring of the Spirit when we know that the Spirit has already been given to us in sacramental baptism. The "newness" then is of a particular quality: we are concerned here with a new coming of the Spirit already present, of an "outpouring" which does not come from outside, but springs up from within. One thinks immediately of the words of Jesus: "If anyone is thirsty, let him come to me, whoever believes in me, let him drink. As Scripture says: 'Streams of living water shall flow out from within him.'" And St. John adds: "He was speaking of the Spirit which believers in him would receive later" (Jn. 7,

37–38). These are images of a springing up of life, an opening out, an action of the Spirit which releases and frees latent interior energies. It is a question of a deeper awareness of the presence and the power of the Holy Spirit.

A theologian, Francis A. Sullivan, professor at the Gregorian University in Rome, defines the experience as follows: "A religious experience which initiates a decisively new awareness of the all powerful presence of God, working in one's life, which working usually involves one or more charismatic gifts." [11]

As we grope for words we discover how difficult it is to express the inexpressible, especially when we are speaking of the mystery of God's actions. Different expressions are being used to define this experience of baptism in the Spirit: the grace of actualizing gifts already received, a release of the Spirit, a manifestation of baptism, a coming to life of the gift of the Spirit received at confirmation, profound receptivity or docility to the Holy Spirit. By whatever name we call it, those who have had this experience speak of it as a very special grace, as a renewal of their spiritual life accompanied by a feeling of peace and joy of a kind hitherto unknown. They esteem this grace as a revitalizing of the sacramental graces they have already received, conferred at baptism, then at confirmation, as well as at the reception of the other sacraments: penance, the eucharist, marriage, ordination. This Renewal is experienced as a release of the latent potentials of the Spirit whose desire is to lead each one of us to the full realization of his own vocation, be this lay or religious. It is a new and more developed awareness of our true Christian identity which only faith can reveal to us; and which brings alive this faith, giving it a new reality and an awakened eagerness to spread the Gospel.

Let us try to make this analysis more precise by investigating three complementary points.

a. *The link between the Spirit and the charisms.*

First of all, we must observe clearly, it seems to me, the link between the Holy Spirit and his manifestations, so that we concentrate our attention, not on the gifts, but on the Giver. We know the prayer of Augustine: "Not your gifts, Lord, but you!" The gifts are nothing more than the shining rays of the Spirit who is himself the Gift *par excellence,* the Gift who contains all other gifts within himself. We must abide with this Spirit as a person in his living and radiant reality. The manifestations of the Spirit are the Holy Spirit at work. This action or motion of God is infinitely supple, discreet and supremely free. The Spirit blows where, when, and how he wills. At all costs we must not make "things" out of the Spirit's gifts, treat them as objects, bequests to be handed out to the different persons who have been left legacies in a will! The gifts are related to the Giver as are the rays of sunlight to the sun: they are not to be identified with him; but neither have they subsistence apart from him.

The Spirit is inseparable from his gifts. When I receive him I receive the fullness of all that is his. And this fullness is itself not something static, but dynamic. This does not mean that all the gifts received along with him who is their Source, are manifested, nor that they are manifested in the same way or at the same time.

The visibility of the gifts, the manner in which they are exercised, will differ, not only from person to person, but also, in each person the action of the Spirit modifies the use to which the gifts are put. I do not possess the gifts as my personal property, as I might objects in a drawer. It is rather I who am possessed by the Spirit who moves me and leads me according to the good pleasure of his boundless love, and in accordance with the degree of faith, hope and love he finds in me. The Spirit who gives me strength today for a particular mission, can tomorrow confide to me another. He is able also to manifest himself in me, not only in one gift, but in many, either successively or all at once. We must continually correct our human way of thinking about God, our tendency to measure and catalogue his gifts. St. Paul draws up with the greatest freedom a list of charisms. He gives different enumerations of them, and does not consider any one of them either definitive or exhaustive; they are samples, not a complete catalogue. If he sometimes presents the gifts as though each person received one gift for the common good, we should not unduly press this "distributive" image which makes no pretense of conveying all the nuances of the manysided action of the Spirit. Paul is first of all preoccupied, when he writes to the Corinthians, with good order in the liturgical assemblies; he is not attempting to describe the interior action of the Holy Spirit. One sentence sums up his thought: "To each one is given the manifestation of the Spirit for the collective good" (1 Cor. 12, 7): the converging of all the gifts builds up the Church.

b. *The Holy Spirit as initially present.*

The second observation touches upon what I would call our "futurist" language. Whenever we speak of a new coming of the Holy Spirit within the soul of someone baptized, we must also speak in the perspective of the Spirit as "already received." In other words, we must assume the fundamental fact that a baptized Christian has already received the fullness of the Holy Spirit. The Spirit is not still on his way, he is already radically present from the very beginning of the Christian life, even if awareness of this reality is not present until later, when the child, who has now become an adult, ratifies, one hopes, the meaning and consequences of his baptism. The Spirit of God is in a baptized person. The promise of God is accomplished; the Christian soul is a dwelling place of the Blessed Trinity.

Consequently holiness is not a long climb toward some far off and inaccessible peak. Christian sanctity is given from the very beginning. Strictly speaking we have not to become holy, but to remain so: we must become what we already are. We have received the Spirit of holiness within us as a pledge and firstfruits. Now we must be faithful to this and, in all fidelity, cultivate the latent resources within us with all their potential and all their "nuclear energy."

In the course of the Christian life, each sacrament extends the rays of the Spirit's action, filling us more and more in both our being and our doing. Baptism is the primal source; it enables the fields to be irrigated and the waters to be channelled. This is the slow process which christianizes little by little the faithful Christian.

When the sacrament of confirmation is conferred upon a child, we have to say to him, at one and the same time: "You are going to receive the Holy Spirit" and "You have already received him." Confirmation is not some supplement to baptism; it confirms baptism.

During the consecration to the episcopacy, the bishop who is consecrating says to the future bishop, as he lays hands on him: "Receive the Holy Spirit. . . ." Here we have an investiture marking a more spectacular action of the Holy Spirit who nevertheless had been already received. The same applies during ordination to the priesthood and the diaconate.

During the Liturgy of Advent we pray, again and again, to the Father to send his Son, as though the Son had not yet become incarnate. During the Liturgy of Pentecost when we ask God to send his Spirit, we are conscious of his previous presence, for in practically the same breath, we call the Spirit the guest of our souls. The Liturgy speaks of the realities of our faith in this evocative manner, without creating any confusion.

We must interpret charismatic language in the same way. The Holy Spirit does not arrive unexpectedly from outside to perfect his work, putting a finishing touch here and there. The temptation is great to speak of God doing something absolutely new, unheard of before and reserved for our times. If we do so, we introduce discontinuity and an arbitrary quality in God's action. We should keep in mind the continuity and God's fidelity to himself. We would not say, for example, that today, all of a sudden, Jesus has decided to give us the Eucharist; his gift is abiding, it is for us to accept it. In the same way the Holy Spirit is an abiding gift; it is for us to let him work in us, "both the will and the action" (Phil. 2, 13). It is we ourselves who, in a mysterious interaction of grace and freedom, make it possible for him to perform a new action, to take a deeper possession of us and to overcome the hindrances and obstacles caused by our sins, our stubbornness, our hesitation. "Do not extinguish the Spirit, do not sadden the Spirit"—these are the imperatives of the Christian life.

When the action of the Holy Spirit becomes more effective in us, it is not that the Spirit has suddenly awakened like some dormant volcano unexpectedly come to life. It is we who are awakened to his presence by a combined movement of his grace, a deeper faith, a more living hope, a more burning love.

This question of a "new" sending of the Son or the Holy Spirit has long been meditated upon by the great mystics and theologians of the Church. St. Thomas distinguishes the visible sending of the Son and the Holy Spirit at the Incarnation and Pentecost from the invisible sending which takes place in the life of each Christian.[12] Quoting a famous phrase of St. Augustine, he too places the reality of "sending" in the context of a new perception: "The Son is sent whenever he is perceived." St. Thomas explains, " 'Perception' in this context signifies that perception which is experience." Then, speaking of the invisible mission of the Holy Spirit, St. Thomas writes these significant words: "We should say that the invisible mission also takes place when there is a growth in virtue or an increase in grace. . . . But the invisible mission is particularly evident in that increase of grace by which someone moves to a new state or a new act of grace. As, for example, when someone progresses in the grace of working miracles or of prophecy, or when in the fervor of love he gives himself up to martyrdom or renounces his goods, or undertakes any difficult work." [13]

At baptism we all receive the fullness of the Holy Spirit, the layman as well as the priest, bishop or pope. The Holy Spirit cannot be received more or less, any more than a host is more or less consecrated. Each of us receives the Spirit of God with the charisms which are necessary for the fulfillment of our individual mission. Adapting the formula of tradition we may say: "The Spirit is sent whenever he is perceived."

c. *The Spirit as an abiding power.*

The Holy Spirit is the soul of the Christian life, not only at its beginnings, but throughout the whole of its growth and development. The Scriptures constantly recall that the Spirit is power and that we should have the courage to rely on his strength which can lift us above ourselves if we give it freedom within us.

It is remarkable to see how St. Paul or St. Luke associate the Holy Spirit with power.

In Luke, we read of Mary: "The Holy Spirit will come upon you, and the power of the Most High will cover you with its shadow" (Lk. 1, 35). St. Luke says practically the same concerning the apostles, quoting Jesus: "And now, I am sending upon you my Father's promised gift. Stay in the city, until you are clothed with power from on high" (Lk. 24, 49). And again, ". . . you will receive power when the Holy Spirit comes on you, and then you will be my witnesses . . ." (Acts 1, 8). It is important to note here that it is not the apostles left to themselves who are to be witnesses, but the apostles under the movement of the Holy Spirit. By themselves they were able to testify, as direct eye-witnesses, to certain events concerning the resurrection, but it is only by the power of the Spirit that they could give witness to the meaning of that resurrection. In the prophetic light received from the Spirit, they were able to interpret the events of salvation; the power of their word comes from the Spirit.

St. Paul pronounces this blessing, full of confidence in the Holy Spirit, upon his Roman readers: "May the God of hope fill you with all joy and peace by your faith in him, until by the power of the Holy Spirit, you overflow with hope" (Rom. 15, 13). To the Corinthians he reveals a bit of his own experience: "Far from relying on any power of my own, I came among you in great 'fear and trembling' and in my speeches and the sermons that I gave, there were none of the persuasive arguments that belong to philosophy: only a demonstration of the power of the Spirit" (1 Cor. 2, 3–4).

These are expressions of Christian faith. This power of the Holy Spirit is not reserved only for the apostles, it is an integral part of the heritage given to all of us. If we would dare believe in it, we would find our discouragement in the service of the Lord swept away, and we would cease looking upon the spiritual life as a prolonged ascetic effort which we must endure by our own force of will. We would see it, rather for what it is: the work of the Spirit in and with us, supporting us with his unfailing presence and power.

Many of those who have obeyed the norms laid down by the masters of the spiritual life have to admit that, after years of sincere effort, they still remain mediocre. They cannot maintain the effort required nor find the energy necessary for the daily struggle. The mountain of perfection seems too high, and the price to pay too demanding. They have given up the climb to the summit and try to remain content with the foothills. It is precisely for such discouraged people that faith in the Holy Spirit can be an experience of the fact that, though discipline of the will is indispensable in a true Christian life, this discipline is neither the origin nor the center of asceticism. An asceticism based on our own will power cannot take us far. Faith in the present, active power of the Spirit does not dispense us from asceticism, but it sets it in true perspective—in a secondary place. Such a faith can show us that holiness is primarily an "assumption" rather than an "ascension." That is to say, it is God who reaches out to us and bears us aloft. This is a truth that we must learn and learn again.

The Meaning and Relevance of this Experience

The fresh breath of the Spirit, too,
has come to awaken latent energies
within the Church,
to stir up dormant charisms, and to
infuse a sense of vitality and joy.
It is this sense of vitality and joy
which makes the Church youthful and
relevant in every age,
and prompts her to proclaim joyously
her eternal message to each new epoch.[1]

POPE PAUL VI

The religious experience which I have just described poses for all those in positions of leadership in the Church a delicate problem of discernment, which we should discuss before moving on to determine the meaning and relevance of the experience itself.

I. TO BE PRESENT AND DISCERN.

Faced with what has happened and is, we must admit, in the nature of a surprise of the Holy Spirit, we could adopt different attitudes: one, critical, but disposed to be favourable; two, distrustful and therefore not disposed to listen; three, uncritical enthusiasm.

At the Council, we heard a great deal about our duty to read "the signs of the times," that is, to hear God's voice speaking to us through the needs of our fellowmen. We should never neglect this vital task. But there is another duty: that of reading the signs that the Lord himself puts in the heavens, so to speak, like the star of Bethlehem which led the Magi to the discovery of Christ. Confronted with what may be an intervention of God, we have first and foremost to put ourselves in a state of generous receptivity. We know already that the ways of God are not our ways, nor are his thoughts our thoughts. We know, too, that God is compassion and that our very distress is, in his eyes, a call for help. Well, the Church has never known a more critical moment in her history. From a human point of view, there is no help on the horizon. We do not see from where salvation can come, unless from HIM; there is no salvation except in his name.

At this moment, we see in the sky of the Church manifestations of the Holy Spirit's action which seem to be like those known to the early Church. It is as though the Acts of the Apostles and the letters of St. Paul were coming to life again, as if God were once more breaking into our history.

The Holy Father, in the words quoted at the heading of this chapter, speaks of latent energies which are awakening, of dormant charisms arising once again. He is not limiting his remark to what is called the Charismatic Movement, but neither are his words chosen at random.

We have an instinctive fear of God intruding into our affairs, even if they are going badly. We stiffen in the face of any interference from outside; we regard it as estrangement, and we fear a wisdom that does not obey our laws. The very idea of intervention on the part of God makes us uneasy. We usually steer clear of those passages in the

Bible which do not conform to our categories. God's nearness disturbs us. We take exception whenever his action gets too close and upsets our daily routine. Our real fear, however, ought to be that we may not recognize God's coming in time, that we may not be there when he knocks at our door.

If there is an area where one can touch and feel the need for a teaching body in the Church, enlightened by theology and confirmed by tradition and a tried wisdom, it is in the vast and delicate domain of the spiritual life. I once heard the episcopal office defined as "the charism of discerning charisms." This is even more than a definition: it is a call to assume our responsibilities in the service of the Church and not shirk them. At this moment, whether they like it or not, the shepherds are required to speak out and give direction.

The vitality of the Charismatic Renewal in the United States obliged the American episcopacy to take a stand. In 1969 they appointed a commission headed by Bishop Alexander Zaleski to report to the Episcopal Conference. There have been other favorable signs. Bishop Joseph McKinney, auxiliary bishop of Grand Rapids, has become de facto, a link between the episcopacy and the Charismatic Renewal, and has recently been appointed a consultor to the Pastoral Research and Practices Committees. As I write, the American Episcopal Conference has confided to this committee, under the direction of Archbishop John Quinn of Tulsa, the task of elaborating more specific guidelines. Many priests and some bishops are present regularly at prayer meetings and other functions connected with the Charismatic Renewal, and finally we could mention the express and positive reference to the Renewal in an official document of the Church in the United States dealing with the spirituality of the American priesthood.[2]

At this present moment, every day, a number of bishops throughout the world are called on to exercise their own

charism of discernment in this matter. They cannot take
refuge in a policy of "wait and see" because if in the
absence of the shepherd, the sheep should wander, the
fault will be his not theirs. However, the bishop's charism
is not automatic. For the exercise of his gift of discernment, he must have accurate information on every aspect
of the question, from as many first-hand sources as
possible.

He must avoid making rapid decisions based on first
impressions or perhaps on unfortunate incidents which are
bound to occur wherever human beings are involved. His
charism of discernment relies basically on prudence, and
prudence requires that he goes to the bottom of things and
weighs the respective value of the evidence he hears.
Human prudence usually "plays for safety": it must give
way to supernatural prudence, which is anxious not to
misunderstand an action of God in and for his Church.
Prayer, which opens our minds to God, is indispensable
also to recognize his action, no matter how much it runs
counter to our poor human wisdom.

In regard to the Charismatic Renewal particularly, in
some way or other, direct experience is needed if we are to
make a balanced judgment—there must be an understanding of this reality "from the inside."

The presence of the bishops can take different forms,
but there must be some sort of real support if the
Charismatic Renewal is to maintain a healthy orientation
and authentic integration in the Church. No one who was
there can ever forget the spontaneous ovation of some
twenty-two thousand people when the speaker at the
International Conference at Notre Dame, in 1973, stressed
the unanimous desire to be in close union with the
shepherds of the Church.

It seems to me that bishops must answer the call
addressed to them in so moving a manner by their flock.
The paradox is that the Charismatic Renewal, which

would seem to be "outside the structure" and so independent of official initiative, is precisely the one reality in the modern Church which is calling out to the hierarchy for that kind of leadership and discernment which corresponds exactly to the grace the Lord has given to the sherpherds of his flock.

We must remember, however, that being present and giving direction are not the same as "taking over" in an authoritarian manner. Any legislation at this moment which is too rigid would be premature and stifle the spontaneity and life of the Renewal. Does not the Lord remind us that at times we should let the weeds spring up with the wheat so as not to ruin the future harvest? The harvest promises to be indeed rich. As bishops, our task is to respect the healthy liberty of the children of God, while putting ourselves at their service as "fellow workers for their happiness" (2 Cor. 1, 24). The spiritual wisdom of the Church and of the saints, nourished by her, can be of immense benefit to all.

This was the tenor of the address which the Holy Father gave to the representatives at the international meeting of the Charismatic Renewal, held at Grottaferrata on October 9–11, 1973. After the general audience on October 10, he received a group of leaders, along with Archbishop James Hayes of Halifax, Nova Scotia, and Bishop Joseph McKinney, auxiliary of Grand Rapids. I give here the complete text of his address, as it appeared in the English edition of *L'Osservatore Romano* and I add, in italics, some comments the Holy Father made spontaneously to the group that met with him. These are reported in *New Covenant*, December, 1973:

> "We are very interested in what you are doing.
> We have heard so much about what is happening
> among you. And we rejoice. We have many
> questions to ask you but there is no time."

And now a word to the members of the Grottaferrata congress:

"We rejoice with you, dear friends, at the renewal of spiritual life manifested in the Church today, in different forms and in various environments. Certain common notes appear in this renewal: the taste for deep prayer, personal and in groups, a return to contemplation and an emphasizing of praise of God, the desire to devote oneself completely to Christ, a great availability for the calls of the Holy Spirit, more assiduous reading of the Scripture, generous brotherly devotion, the will to make a contribution to the service of the Church. In all that, we can recognize the mysterious and discreet work of the Spirit, who is the soul of the Church.

"Spiritual life consists above all in the exercise of the virtue of faith, hope and charity. It finds its foundation in the profession of faith. The latter has been entrusted to the pastors of the Church to keep it intact and help it to develop in all the activities of the Christian community. The spiritual lives of the faithful, therefore, come under the active pastoral responsibility of each bishop in his diocese. It is particularly opportune to recall this in the presence of these ferments of renewal which arouse so many hopes.

"Even in the best experiences of renewal, moreover, weeds may be found among the good seed. So a work of discernment is indispensable; it devolves upon those who are in charge of the Church, "to whose special competence it belongs, not indeed to extinguish the Spirit, but to test all things and hold fast to that which is good" (cf. 1 Th 5, 12 and 19–21) (*Lumen Gentium*, 12). In this way the common good of the Church, to which the gifts of the Spirit are ordained (cf. 1 Cor. 12, 7), makes progress.

"We will pray for you that you may be filled with the fullness of the Spirit and live in His joy and in His holiness. We ask for your prayers and we will remember you in Mass." [3]

II. JUDGING THE TREE BY ITS FRUITS.

Because I have had extended personal contact in the

United States and elsewhere with the leaders and theologians of this religious awakening, I would like to try here to delineate the factors that I find constant in this Renewal. If the charisms, as such, often escape our capacity for discernment, the fruits of the Spirit about which Paul speaks are always easy to recognize (Gal. 5, 22–23).

The Lord told us to judge a tree by its fruits, and this is a solid criterion. Recent investigations, emanating from completely different parts of the world, have arrived at approximately the same positive conclusions. The critical but warm appraisal of Pastor Appia, the official liaison between the Protestant Federation of France and the Catholic Church, is important. Based on personal and extensive research conducted with a group of French delegates, it is amazingly similar in its results to the research that I have conducted myself along with others interested. I give here, without attempting to determine their order of precedence, some of the striking and widespread effects of the Charismatic Renewal.

CHRISTOCENTRICITY.

First of all, one notices that the spirituality of the Renewal is clearly oriented towards Jesus with whom is formed a living, experienced, and intimate relationship. Jesus Christ, "he who baptizes in the Holy Spirit" (Jn. 1, 33) is in the foreground. A close person-to-person encounter develops in which the Lord Jesus himself begins the dialogue and invites a response. Often such a meeting means the discovery of what Christianity really is. It is not an ideology or another "ism," but a meeting with the living person Jesus, the supreme reality who is recognized as Saviour, Master, Shepherd, Way, Truth and Life, Alpha and Omega both in himself and for the world. We should notice here that the Jesus who is at the heart of this

Renewal is the Jesus of our faith and not the Jesus whom one finds too often in some circles of the "Jesus Revolution" or the "Jesus People," reduced to purely human dimensions. He who concerns us is the Jesus of our faith: the Son of God become man, God of God, the Word with and in God, in whom there lives bodily the fullness of the Godhead, who has suffered for us, showing us the way, to whom all power in heaven and on earth had been entrusted, and who leads us into the fullness of his inheritance, the most Holy Spirit.

This intimacy with the Lord, in a direct relationship instead of through a curtain of ideas, quite naturally gives rise to a second characteristic: a new understanding of prayer. It is one thing to speak *about* God, another to speak *to* God. And yet another to *listen* to God in a deep silence.

THE LIFE OF PRAYER.

In the Charismatic Renewal, one witnesses a deepening of the life of prayer both on the individual and communal level. The soul seems to open to a more pervasive action of the Holy Spirit who "alone explores even the depths of God" (1 Cor. 2, 11), giving us access to the Father (see Eph. 2, 18) and causing us to share in the life of the Trinity. One sees a zest for the things of the Spirit, an invitation to increase and prolong prayer and so be the better aware of the presence and light of the Holy Spirit. This prayer which is sometimes silent, sometimes softly murmured, sometimes sung in a spirit of recollection, joy, and ease, has a special quality because it is spontaneous. It is a rediscovery, to the letter, of what Paul wrote to the Ephesians: "Let the Holy Spirit fill you: speak to one another in psalms, hymns and songs; sing and make music in your hearts to the Lord; and in the name of our Lord

Jesus Christ give thanks every day for everything to our God and father" (Eph. 5, 18–20).

Also striking is the quality of this prayer. Without eliminating intercession and petition, what dominates is the prayer of praise which in the past we omitted all too often in our devotions. "Praise the Lord" is very much more than a multiplied refrain: like Alleluia's at Easter-time, it expresses a love of God in and for himself.

The spontaneity of this prayer, expressed by rhythmic movement, clapping of hands, hands raised or joined altogether in a sign of unity is especially appreciated by young people. It helps those who lend themselves to it, to step out of their individualism, their inhibitions and their excessive cerebralism.

Sometimes people object to this as being too emotional. It is worthwhile analyzing this objection more closely. For if someone objects to the emotional character of a particular style of prayer, it can well be that he feels himself threathened by its personal quality. We are so accustomed to formalism, ritualism, and conventionalism, that deeply personal prayer can present a challenge to our inhibitions. We are afraid to be ourselves before God and before one another and hence we resort to a defense mechanism which labels as "emotionalism" what in reality is an authentic personal quality of prayer. We tend to avoid emotion in our relations with God, or at least we prefer to depersonalize prayer, just as we have today stripped and laid bare so many of our churches.

Perhaps it is time to react to some degree against the abuse we have made of those words of our Lord inviting us to worship "in spirit and in truth." After all, the Son of God became man, and his religion fully embraces and heals all that is really human. A dehumanized spiritual life goes against the logic of the Incarnation: Jesus did not die to save souls—he died to save men.

Another aspect of Charismatic prayer is love for the Scriptures. The reading of the Holy Scripture plays a large role at prayer meetings and in the personal and communal life of the faithful who are in contact with the Renewal. People are rediscovering the Bible and there is a genuine thirst for the word of God, not so much on the level of exegetical research—though this is not excluded—as on that of daily life. Jesus said: "My words are spirit and life" (Jn. 6, 63). The words of the Lord are becoming nourishment for his people. I think of Jeremiah: "When your words came, I devoured them: your word was my delight and the joy of my heart" (Jer. 15, 16).

This Renewal contributes something to advancement in exegesis not by providing new answers, but by asking new questions. We are invited to examine the text more closely in function of our daily lives. The grace of the Renewal is, in this respect, the grace of a deeper reading of Scripture, a deeper grasp of its reality; it is prayerfully meditated on and shared, but always with reference to concrete situations. This makes the role of an experienced guide all the more valuable in helping people to avoid a fundamentalist approach or excessive subjectivity.

I consider, too, that this spontaneous mode of prayer is a particular grace for the Church today, coming at a moment when the popular prayer life of the faithful—holy hour, novenas, rosaries, stations of the Cross, etc.—has almost disappeared, leaving a void that needs to be filled.

This mode of prayer, which is intermediary between purely private and strictly liturgical prayer, can be of great help in renewing the spiritual life in the home and in the most diverse types of communities: parishes, schools, movements, religious and monastic houses. Spontaneous Charismatic prayer can make a great contribution towards rediscovering the true meaning of prayer as a reality which springs up from life, varying according to individual situations. It lends itself by its very suppleness to deepening certain moments of the liturgy. It is open to all the manifestations of the Spirit and thus naturally becomes itself a symphony of prayer, enriched by the wonderful diversity of the gifts of God.

PRAYING AND SPEAKING IN TONGUES.

A newcomer to a prayer meeting is often intrigued to hear, from time to time, one person—or the whole group—beginning to pray or sing in tongues. His first impression is one of uneasiness prompted by this sponta-neous verbal expression, in which syllables succeed one another, forming phrases that are unintelligible. It is important to understand "glossalalia," neither minimizing nor exaggerating the importance of this mode of prayer. It is not a miracle; it is not pathological.

Not a miracle.

Charismatics of many denominations, but especially classical Pentecostals, consider glossalalia as the indisput-able sign that one has received the "baptism in the Holy Spirit." And they also hold that it is an infused gift enabling someone to pray in a real language which he himself does not understand. This we cannot accept. I have already shown how such a viewpoint is incompatible with Catholic theology. But we do not exclude the possibility that in certain rare cases it has happened, for we believe in miracles, and such a phenomenon would pertain to the order of miracle.

Not pathological.

At the other extreme, we find people, especially those who are to some degree familiar with psychiatry, shrug-ging their shoulders speaking of pathological conditions:

emotionalism, mass hysteria, infantile regression, etc. This is not the view of solid scientific investigation, nor is it that of one of the most qualified men in this field, William J. Samarin, professor of anthropology and linguistics at the University of Toronto. Professor Samarin concludes a long, extended study, conducted in many countries, by declaring that this phenomenon contains nothing abnormal nor pathological, and he offers proofs.[4]

If praying in tongues is, then, neither miraculous nor pathological, how are we to assess it?

What then is glossalalia?

We should first recognize that we are dealing with something that is referred to in the Scriptures: there are, indeed, about thirty allusions to praying in tongues. In the New Testament, we have the witness of Acts (2, 4–11; 10, 46; 19, 6), the letters of St. Paul (1 Cor. 12, 30; 13, 1; 14, 2.39), and also the promise of Jesus in the Gospel of St. Mark (16, 7). There are undoubtedly exegetical problems, but this should not blind us to the simple fact that the New Testament speaks of this phenomenon as real and relatively frequent. St. Paul says that this "gift" is the least important in the hierarchy of gifts; he also says that he possesses it himself and wishes it for others, though he stresses that, in public worship, moderation must always be respected. We cannot say then, that there is no biblical evidence for the existence of this gift. It is also found in the living tradition of the Church, widely diffused at the beginning and then, to a more limited degree, in monasteries and in the lives of saints.

I would like to contribute here some personal reflections, which claim to be neither definitive nor exhaustive.

We should note at the outset that, in virtue of baptism, every Christian has received the Holy Spirit and thus, potentially, all the gifts of the Spirit. The visible manifestation of a gift, its active exercise, reveals its presence but it does not create the gift. A fundamentalistic reading of the New Testament might induce one to treat these gifts of God as "objects," something exterior to ourself. The importance of speaking in tongues is not minimized if we situate it on a natural plane, which can assume a supernatural charter through the intention which animates it. Further, we should remember that everything, in a sense, is a gift: "everything is grace."

This form of non-discursive prayer—a preconceptual expression of spontaneous prayer—is within the reach of everybody and remains always under control. It is a verbal expression independant of any specific linguistic structure. This manner of expression, known to other civilizations, is less a stranger to ourselves than is supposed. Think, in the Gregorian chant of the jubilation inherent in the prolonged "A" sound at the end of the Alleluia's. Think too, of how a little child, before having learned to speak coherently, adopts spontaneously these varied sounds and unintelligible syllables to express his joy.

Someone has said that praying in tongues is in relation to discursive prayer, as is abstract art to figurative art; the comparison, I think, throws some light.

The gift of tongues has also been compared to the gift of tears. Anyone who feels strong emotion is able to cry; actors can shed tears whenever the script calls for them. This is natural. But there is also a gift of tears, recognized by a spiritual tradition, that goes far back in time. Moreover, in the Ritual, there is a prayer for this gift. It is a profound religious experience in which one gives expression to the inexpressible, when moved by a sense of compunction, adoration or gratitude before God. These tears, if we analyze them, are no different from any others, but their religious significance goes far beyond the physical phenomenon. The analogy with tongues is appropriate.

RELIGIOUS VALUE OF PRAYING IN TONGUES.

Why Pray in Tongues?

Having tried to see in perspective this mode of religious expression, we should attempt some evaluation of its spiritual value. There are numerous testimonies—and I would join my own to them—which witness to the fact that this mode of prayer brings a freedom from spiritually inhibiting bonds, which block our relationship with God and with our fellowmen and makes us find a whole new sense of liberation.

If, at the outset, a person accepts this act of humility—the risk of appearing foolish or childish—he soon discovers the joy of praying in a way that transcends words and human reasoning, bringing great peace and an openness to spiritual communication with others.

Nor are other forms of prayer excluded. Moreover, it can be practiced alone or in a group. When, in a prayer meeting, it takes the form of an improvised chant in tongues, it can assume, in musical terms, a rare beauty as well as a religious depth by which no one who listens without prejudice can fail to be impressed.

If St. Paul treats this gift as the least of all—though he used it himself—might this not be because it is, in a sense, a way that leads to the other gifts, a small doorway as it were, which can only be entered by stooping: like the door into the Church of the Nativity at Bethlehem? Humility and a childlike spirit characterize the Kingdom of God: "If you do not become as little children. . . ." We know this saying of Jesus, and it has considerable relevance here. The gift of tongues, which has nothing to do with the intellect, makes a breach in the "reserve" we assume as a system of defense. It helps us cross a threshold and, in doing so, attain a new freedom in our surrender to God. This surrender hands over body and soul to the action of the Holy Spirit. It is only a first step by which we learn how to yield to the other gifts, but nonetheless it is precious because it gives expression, in its own way, to the inner freedom of the children of God.

Karl Barth once defined glossalalia as an attempt to express the inexpressible, and St. Paul says that "the Spirit intercedes with unspeakable groanings" (Rom. 8, 26). It is to this mysterious, inarticulate prayer of the Spirit that we unite ourselves, leaving to the Holy Spirit the role of glorifying God and giving thanks for a love "which is beyond all knowledge." In psychological terms, we could say that it is the voice of the subconscious rising to God, finding a manner of praying which is analogous to other expressions of our subconscious in dreams, laughter, tears, painting, or dance. This prayer within the depths of our being heals at a profound yet often perceptible level hidden psychological wounds that impede the full development of our interior life.

Let us admit it: we are terribly complicated when it comes to giving outward expression to our deep religious feelings before God or in front of others. Even priests and religious know at what cost they reveal themselves at any spiritual depth to those with whom they live, and how often community life is little more than a superficial juxtaposition of individual lives. We have been ossified by formalism and ritualism. Our liturgical gatherings have only begun to awaken to the meaning of communal liturgy after centuries of passivity. But though a thaw has set in, we have yet to experience the warmth and enthusiasm that should characterize our liturgical celebrations in community. Only recently the Pope again warned us against routine in prayer and the misuse of ready-made formulas.

At this very time, we are awakening to new dimensions of bodily expression and communication with one another. There is growing interest too in ways of life and prayer that derive from oriental philosophies, and in the

practices of non-Europeans who are less rigid than ourselves. Our young people naturally gravitate in this
direction.

We should not be surprised then to see this revival of a
practice which is in no way foreign to our authentic
religious tradition. When someone has once experienced
this freedom in expressing deep-down spiritual feelings, he
senses the need to share with others what he feels. It seems
quite natural and helpful that we should be able to praise,
adore, glorify and love God with all the means at our
disposal—using all the strings of our harp. Among these
means, the gift of tongues for those who have grasped its
significance, is an integral factor.

Speaking in tongues thus conceived is spiritual enrichment; far from being an archaism, it is a factor of renewal
on more than one level: that is why I do not hesitate to
count it among the fruits of grace. But it is the task of
theologians to study this question more deeply, not only in
texts, but by experiencing it in prayer groups.

PRAYER AND SOCIAL ACTION.

The fear has also been expressed that this insistence on
prayer may cultivate in some a pietistic dichotomy between the spiritual life and one's responsibilities to society
and, consequently, an alienation from the world. To have
faith, it has been said with justice, means not only to lift
one's eyes to heaven to contemplate God, but also to look
at the earth and see it with the eyes of Christ. This danger
of turning in on oneself or limiting one's attention only to
the group, has not escaped the notice of the leaders in the
Charismatic Renewal. They have drawn attention to it in a
series of articles in *New Covenant*[5] and during the international leaders' meeting at Grottaferrata (October, 1973).

Still more than by these warnings, the danger is
efficaciously forestalled and counterbalanced by social

initiatives of the most diverse forms, which have been undertaken by many prayer groups. It is true that, in general, this social responsibility is exercised in a direct and personal way toward those who are within immediate reach rather than on a vast social scale. However, the one does not exclude the other and communion in prayer should normally lead to a communion among all men, with all the social and political responsibility this implies. Mexico is a striking example of this integration because there the Charismatic Renewal began among the groups most committed to the social apostolate.

A SENSE OF THE CHURCH.

There is another characteristic of the Renewal: love for the Church, respect for her spiritual motherhood, her institutional dimension and her sacramental life. Because it is not aligned with either "right" or "left" ideology, the Charismatic Renewal unites within itself the most divergent tendencies that we find in Christianity today; polarization is overcome by a living and authentic brotherly love. Meeting in prayer provides a powerful antidote to the divisions which set us at variance. In our day that is quite an accomplishment! Generally, within the Renewal one breathes a fresh air, unpolluted by conflicts, grudges, or bitterness. People are intent upon building the Church of God, and they want to build together on the only true foundation: Jesus, the Lord and Savior.[6]

Obviously we cherish the hope that this truly Catholic sense will last and grow within all the Charismatic groups. Elitism would be fatal: there are no "super-Christians."

III. THE MEANING AND RELEVANCE OF THIS EXPERIENCE.

Judging the tree by its fruits is a valuable criterion that can be applied to everything that purports to be a work of the Spirit. We can only rejoice at the many manifestations of the Spirit which comply so well with this criterion.

If I have spoken of the Renewal as a privileged manifestation of the Spirit at this moment in the Church, it is not because I consider it an exclusive reality destined to replace everything else. I hope that no one will misrepresent my thought in this regard. However, I do believe, with all my heart, that we are in the presence here of a very special grace for the Church, provided we know how to receive it, guide its growth from within, preserve it from counterfeits which the evil one will certainly produce, and let it penetrate, by a sort of osmosis, into the heart of our collective and individual attitudes and behaviour.

I. THE "NORMAL" CHRISTIAN.

Every movement of the Holy Spirit challenges us to question ourselves as to our own cooperation with grace and our own Christian identity.

For me, the most striking aspect of the experience that I have analyzed here is the fact that it compels me to look with new eyes at texts in the New Testament that I thought I knew. As I suddenly see manifestations of the Holy Spirit, especially in the Acts, I have to ask myself: "Were those Christians of the early Church exceptional, inimitable beings, living lives of perfection, who have ceased to exist, or is it that we Christians of today with our weakened faith are really "sub-normal?" I find I have to question myself as to the norms of true Christian fidelity and to look at the quality of my personal adherence to Jesus Christ. Do I really believe the words of Paul: "It is no longer I who live, it is Christ who lives in me" (Gal. 2, 20)? He said this not only of himself but as applicable to every Christian who dares to believe that Jesus Christ wishes to prolong now, in and through him, the life he himself lived among us. This was the explicit promise of

Jesus: "He who believes in me, will also do the works that I do; and greater works than these will he do" (Jn. 14, 12).

This question then obliges us to look afresh at Christianity and within it, at what is most ancient and fundamental: fidelity to the life of Christ in the Holy Spirit with all the visible and . . . invisible consequences that this implies. I know that the surest test of our Christian fidelity is love, but this does not exclude other signs of the presence of the Lord within us, signs which he himself gave (see Mk. 16, 17–18) and which appeared on the morning of Pentecost. As I see certain aspects of early Christianity come to life again, I am to take a look at myself as though in a mirror. I must take the measure of the vitality and breadth of my twentieth century Christian faith as compared with that of the Christians of the first century.

2. "ORDINARY" SANCTITY.

Another striking aspect of the Renewal consists in the fact that the manifestations of the Spirit are found among Christians of every walk of life. The students of Pittsburgh, Ann Arbor, and elsewhere are representative of the ordinary Christian. It is not a question of hermits or "specialists" in search of sanctity: these are rank and file Christians. It recalls to mind the words of the Master concerning his first disciples: "I bless you Father, Lord of heaven and of earth, for hiding these things from the learned and the clever and revealing them to mere children" (Lk. 10, 21).

What we see is an openness to the Spirit and his gifts, not just among those who make a profession of striving for sanctity but among Christians who, wherever they are, simply live their faith. Who would have dared to say a few years ago that the charismatic gifts—prophecy, interpretation, healing, miracles—could be the endowment of any Christian who lived his faith? We thought of these gifts as the monopoly of canonized saints or of those in the process of being canonized. This deserves our attention and thought. We must reconsider our teaching in this regard, and this will have far-reaching consequences. I am amazed when I reflect that Vatican II devoted chapter five of the Constitution *On the Church* to reminding us that the vocation to holiness belongs to all Christians: the Holy Spirit was indeed in our midst with all the power that is his. We need only compare Conciliar teaching with our classical treatises on the spiritual life which meticulously outlined, in accordance with principles laid down by learned men, the degrees of holiness and the "states of perfection." At the foot of the pyramid were the laity; at the top, contemplative monks. Moreover the canons regular of the Lateran were at the top of the canonical ladder. Vatican II insisted strongly that holiness was the vocation of every Christian. This democratization of sanctity did not attract the same attention as other "democratic" reforms, but the call of the Council prevailed. Indeed, I can only rejoice to see in the number of vocations in the most diverse walks of life, the manifold responses to the stirrings of the Holy Spirit.

3. THE PROMISED MANIFESTATIONS OF THE SPIRIT.

Once we really believe that Jesus Christ is living and active in each Christian, it is only natural to conclude that he will continue to manifest himself among us. "Even if you refuse to believe in me," he said to his followers, "at least believe in the works I do" (Jn. 10, 38). These works of Jesus were signs and wonders: the healing of the sick, victory over the forces of evil, prophecy, the interpretation of Scripture, the unique sayings of one who taught with authority and spoke as no man had ever spoken. All of this manifested the power of God in Jesus, and it is normal to find it again in his disciples. There is no break in continuity between the Master who healed the paralytic, and Peter and John who said to the paralytic at the Beautiful Gate: ". . . in the name of Jesus Christ the Nazarene, walk!" (Acts 3, 6). It is the same Lord, the same Spirit.

The difference between ourselves and the early Christians is that their faith was more open and receptive to the riches of the Holy Spirit. With our faith renewed in the power of the Holy Spirit, it is not surprising to see again a flowering of the charismatic gifts.

A theologian, who has a wide experience of the Charismatic Renewal, Father Kilian McDonnell, O.S.B., has compared the gamut of charismatic possibilities to a spectrum which can be numbered A to Z.[7] It is understood, of course, that any such analogy can only be relative and that no one can catalogue the dynamic, multiform, and unpredictable action of God. Along this spectrum he distinguishes two sectors: A to P, and P to Z. Let A to P stand for the ordinary gifts, and P to Z for what are called the extraordinary gifts. Christians, he says, are more or less familiar with section A to P, but they do not expect that the gifts in the second part of the spectrum will be manifested in the normal life of a Christian. As far as ordinary believers are concerned, this sector appears to them as the private domain of some saints and other exceptional persons. They will readily admit that in the early Church the whole spectrum of gifts was manifested in their fullness, but one no longer expects to find these on a large scale among Christians of the twentieth century. This is what has been normally presented in our teaching and no one ever thought it necessary to question it.

There is another illustration that might be helpful. We could compare spiritual charisms, collectively, to great organs with many powerful pipes. Each organ is the instrument of the Holy Spirit: he is both the wind that fills the pipes and the musician who plays the organ. The keys vibrate at the touch of him whom the liturgy calls the "hand" and the "finger of God." To play the organ in a manner that does justice to its power, all the keys must respond to his touch: if some keys are silent, something is wrong. If the Church does not respond to the Holy Spirit with the melody he desires, the fault is not his. It is ours, because we dare not believe that the keys can produce sound at the touch of the musician, if only they do not resist him.

What is lacking in us is a realization of our Christian identity. We dare not believe with an expectant faith that the various gifts of the Spirit are always there for the Church of God. We do not recall often enough that we are rich with the riches of God and that these are ours in faith for the humble asking if we are ready to receive them with confidence. We Christians do not know who we are. We are children of God, heirs to his Kingdom, but we behave as if it were not so. We have at our disposal spiritual treasures which remain buried because their existence is unknown to us, or because we lack the faith to believe that they can be found and used.

Faced with manifestations of the Holy Spirit which, in many cases seem to me to be of unquestionable authenticity, I am forced to read again with fresh insight those texts in the New Testament that speak of the charisms of the Spirit as perfectly normal in the life of the early communities. I knew that the Acts of the Apostles was not just an archaic document, and at the Council I defended the actuality of these charisms. But it is one thing to uphold a thesis which I believe to be valid, and another to be challenged face to face with facts which confirm that thesis. This challenge touches us all. What strikes me most in the events that are taking place now is not their novelty but the resurgence of our original tradition and the rediscovery of our point of departure. And I recall the verse of T. S. Eliot:

"We shall not cease from exploration
And the end of all our exploring
Will be to arrive where we started
And know the place for the first time." [8]

The liturgical renewal brought us back to where we started: the Cenacle at Jerusalem on Holy Thursday. The Charismatic Renewal is calling us to that same Cenacle, on the morning of Pentecost. It is a grace to understand better our beginnings—even if we think we know them—and to become more deeply aware of our Christian identity.

A CURRENT OF GRACE.

To grasp the meaning of the Charismatic Renewal and its true bearing on our lives, we have to avoid two tendencies. First, we should not apply to it ready made categories. Secondly, we should not see in this Renewal just one more movement to be set alongside many others in the Church today, or, worse still, as in competition with them. Rather than a movement, Charismatic Renewal is a moving of the Holy Spirit which can reach all Christians, lay or cleric. It is comparable to a high voltage current of grace which is coursing through the Church. Every Christian is charismatic by definition; the difference lies in our degree of faith, our awareness of this fundamental and necessarily common reality.

We are not speaking of a "movement," if by that we understand a structural organization with membership and fixed obligations. To benefit by this current, there is no need even to join a formal prayer group. Our Lord told us: "Where two or three meet in my name, I shall be there with them" (Mt. 18, 20). If there is only this modest number, there can be community prayer among Christians. The Spirit blows how and where he wills; he does not need the help of an organization to penetrate all classes of society: lay persons in every walk of life, members of religious congregations and orders, all are within his reach. Moreover,—I risk the prediction—he will quietly, on tip-toe, find his way into bishops' residences, episcopal conferences, and . . . Roman synods!

If Christians who have been touched by this experience like to come together to share their faith, their hope, and their renewed fraternal love, if they find joy in sharing spontaneous prayer in an atmosphere in which they feel at ease because they are untroubled by inhibitions or human respect, this does not imply a "church within the Church." It simply means there are Christians who are happy to be Christians together before the Lord and ready to serve others wherever Providence places them.

Let me make a comparison. If I want to learn Spanish, must I enroll in a Berlitz course? No, I can learn Spanish all alone or with the help of records. I can also learn with the help of a Spanish friend who speaks the language: one friend would be enough. That does not mean that a class in a language school, for instance, has not more to offer me. Prayer groups are much the same: they are made up of friends, learning together to speak the language of praise and intercession that Jesus speaks to the Father.

One of the leaders of the Ann Arbor community, Steve Clark, tells us in simple words what the Charismatic Renewal is and what it is not:

"We are not trying to do something special. We are simply trying to live Christianity in the power of the Spirit. . . . The Holy Spirit is indispensable, we are not. . . . We do not want to equate . . . the Charismatic Renewal as it is today with the renewal of the Church. Many other things are happening that are part of God's renewal of his Church. But what we have discovered is a fundamental dimension of any Church renewal. We are coming to learn how the presence of the Holy Spirit in the Church can be brought to consciousness in people in an effective way; we are also learning how yielding to the work of that Spirit can bring results in Christian life. The work of the Holy Spirit is fundamental; that is, it has to be the basis of everything else in Christian life. The rediscovery of the power of the Spirit, then, is a fundamental part of Church renewal. It has to be at the basis of everything else and it will, of necessity, affect everything else . . . worship and liturgy, community, daily life together, service, evangelism." [9]

Father John Haughey's article, reporting the international conference held at Notre Dame in 1973, was entitled, "The Holy Spirit, a Ghost No Longer." [10] In it, Fr. Haughey, after observing that the leaders of the conference were not speaking of a movement, but of the Lord, added, "the more deeply one is associated with it, the less one is concerned about the movement and the more one is concerned about the movements of the Spirit in himself and his faith community."

The ideal espoused by the spontaneously recognized "leaders" of the "movement"—I must enclose in quotation marks these inadequate expressions—is that it should disappear. One American journalist entitled his article "A Movement that Wishes to Die." That is exact: the ambition of the Charismatic Renewal is to eliminate itself as soon as possible, much as, on another level, the biblical or liturgical movements have ceased to be identifiable groups and disappeared into the life of the Church. The ecumenical movement, it is to be hoped, will do the same. The purpose is to disappear when the goal is reached, even as a river loses itself when it merges into the sea.

There are some who through fear of abuses or errors of misdirection, which are always a possibility, would wish to reject something that, in my opinion, carries within it the signs of God. To these I can only quote words spoken by Gamaliel concerning a group of Christians who had been transformed one Pentecost morning:

"So now, I tell you, keep away from these men and let them alone; for if this plan or this undertaking is of men, it will fail; but if it is of God, you will not be able to overthrow them. You might even be found opposing God" (Acts 5, 38–39).

The Holy Spirit and Christian Authenticity

*God has anointed us
marking us with this seal
and giving us the pledge, the Spirit,
that we carry in our hearts.*

2 CORINTHIANS 1, 22

I. WHAT MAKES AN AUTHENTIC CHRISTIAN?

Renewal in the Church is not even conceivable as long as Christians have not found their identity: that famous "identity" about which everyone is talking and for which everyone is searching, forgetting too often that our identity has its source and fulfillment in God. There is indeed nothing more important than to grasp what a normal Christian really is: what it truly means to be baptized. When I say "normal," I mean we should take the "norm" from God and not from the way in which we respond to his grace. It is God, St. Paul tells us, "who has marked us with his seal" (2 Cor. 1, 22) and it is from here we must begin.

The ideal Christian community, as we know, has never existed, even in the better periods of the Church's history.

Before the resurrection, Jesus himself admitted the disciples were mediocre, and if after the resurrection they were models of courage, even in many instances to the point of martyrdom, they did not lose their narrowness of vision and their prejudices. The disputes between Peter and Paul, or Paul and Barnabas, the divisions within the early communities which are mentioned in letters of Paul—especially concerning the Corinthians—show that there never has been an idyllic Christianity.

We must not, then, dream about restoring some lost paradise. However, this is not to imply that the concept of what it means to be truly Christian is vague and ill-defined. There are unmistakable signs which cannot be counterfeited. Even if some fruit on a tree is damaged by grubs, and some of the branches are broken in a storm, I can judge the quality of the fruit from just one that is ripe and tasty. Our Lord spoke of the wheat and the weeds growing in the same field. Human weakness did not prevent the early Church from giving us a picture of genuine Christianity in its beginnings.

If we want to determine its distinctive character, we must be careful not to define the Christian in terms of his response to the needs of the world in which he lives, but rather in those of his specific origin and the mission given him by God. We should read again, in the second chapter of the Acts of the Apostles, the account of Pentecost. We should consider the scene that is described and listen to the dialogue between Peter, the first witness to Christ, and the crowd which is challenged by the message with which he opens his mission.

The upper room had just been shaken by a violent wind, and the Spirit had come down upon the hundred and twenty disciples in the form of tongues of fire. Peter stepped forward with the eleven apostles—this detail is significant—and spoke to the crowd, explaining that these men were not drunk and that the prophecy of Joel was being fulfilled before their eyes: "In the days to come"—it is the Lord who speaks—"I will pour out my spirit on all mankind, and your sons and daughters shall prophesy and your young men shall see visions and your old men dream dreams . . ." (Acts 2, 17). "Cut to the heart" (this detail too, is important), the crowd asked, "What must we do, brothers?" (Acts 2, 37).

Peter's address provides us with the first definition of Christian identity, the unique quality inherent in being a Christian. "What is the first thing we must do?" the crowd asks. Peter's answer is straightforward and simple: "Repent" he said "and each one of you be baptised in the name of Jesus Christ for the forgiveness of your sins, and then you will receive the gift of the Holy Spirit" (Acts 2, 38). Conversion. Baptism. Personal surrender to Christ. Receiving the Holy Spirit. All of Christianity is contained in these words.

CONVERSION AND BAPTISM.

A Christian is radically a "convert."

The first Christians, those of Pentecost morning, had to undergo a complete change of mind and heart, a *metanoia*, also a break with manifold ties. Baptism meant for them: death to the "old man," deliverance, liberation, a new life. The liturgy of adult baptism proclaims the same thing today, and the baptized child who is the adult of tomorrow, will one day be called upon to make the same renunciations and ratify the same commitment. And this is an important pastoral problem to which we will have to revert.

Personal encounter.

A Christian is a changed person, a convert: he has turned away from himself, so as to adhere to Jesus of

Nazareth who, for his sake, died and rose from the dead.
He has made a personal discovery of Jesus, and acknowledged him as the Christ, the unique Son of the Father, the
Anointed One of the Holy Spirit. He has found in Jesus
the Savior and Lord of all mankind. At the heart of every
true surrender to Christ one finds, in one form or another,
an echo of Claudel's cry on the evening of his conversion,
when he suddenly saw Jesus with new eyes: "Now, all of a
sudden, you are Someone!"

A saving encounter.

We must meet Jesus as a real living person, but also as
Saviour. In the world in which we live, the phrase "Jesus,
Saviour" has become a problem. To know that I am saved,
I must know I have been saved from something. But from
what? Faith tells us that Jesus came to save his people
from the Law. St. Paul proclaims over and over again
liberation from a stifling legalism which holds man captive
in a net of formal prescriptions and ritual; in the face of
such slavery he asserts the true freedom of the children of
God.

Faith also teaches that Jesus came to save me from
myself, from sin and death and the forces of evil. All of
this has no meaning for someone who claims that man is
self-sufficient, that sin does not exist, that there is nothing
after death, and who dismisses the power of the evil one as
an outdated myth. Jesus whose name means "Saviour," "is
the one who is to save his people from their sins" (Mt. 1,
21). He cannot be recognized as such unless we know what
it is from which we have been saved. Recently a speaker
on television, who professed to be a Christian, declared: "I
refuse to be 'saved,' I want to be 'liberated.' " He forgot
that salvation and liberation are closely linked. In saving
man from sin, the root of all evil, both individual and
collective, Jesus established the basis of all forms of

liberation of which we are in need. To free the oppressed, to struggle against violence and injustice, are among the blessings of salvation, as the entire Old Testament had already proclaimed.

Encounter with Jesus, the Lord.

To be a true Christian means, furthermore, to have met Jesus personally, as Saviour, and as *Lord.* I must accept Jesus totally, as a reality, the Lord and Master of my life as I live and experience it day by day. He is the incarnate hope of all mankind. Each one of us must somehow recapture that first meeting which St. John describes between Jesus and two disciples who began to follow him along the bank of the Jordan. It is worth reading the passage again:

"Jesus turned around and said to them: 'What are you looking for?' They went straight to the point: 'Where do you live?' The Master replied 'Come and see' " (Jn. 1, 35–39).

This is a meeting in the true sense of the word. In Jesus these men are going to find the answer to all their searching. Their cry, "We have found the Messiah!" is in itself a world of joy. For a Jew, this cry means that all the hopes of his people have been justified, and the covenant between God and Israel fulfilled: "We have found the one for whom our whole soul has been searching."
This is true for every Christian:

– a Christian's particular distinction is that he has met Jesus on his way;
– he has seen his face;
– he has recognized his voice;
– he has heard Jesus call him by name and invite him to be his friend.

Usually, a meeting of this kind is a gradual process, not the work of a day. Jesus let those two disciples walk after him quite a while before he turned round, but he was already with them in their search for him. Their story is ours.

RECEIVING THE HOLY SPIRIT.

Finally, we may say that a Christian is someone who has met Jesus as the one who "baptizes in the Holy Spirit" (Jn. 1, 33).

We should first note the relationship between Jesus and the Spirit. In the very difference of their persons, they are indissolubly united. The name "Christ" signifies "Anointed by the Holy Spirit"; indeed the whole life of Jesus reveals the presence within him of the Spirit. The radiance of his presence shone forth when, at his baptism in the river Jordan, the Holy Spirit came down upon him in the form of a dove. Like a thread, running through the fabric of his life, the presence of the Spirit manifests itself at times of special significance. The Spirit led him into the desert; filled him with jubilation and prayer, inspired in him the love whereby he was subject to the Father's will and, having died and risen from the dead, became the "source of eternal salvation" (Heb. 5, 9).

On the day after the resurrection, Paul tells us, Christ became for us the "life-giving Spirit" (1 Cor. 15, 45), so closely related to one another are the roles of Jesus and the Spirit. The Lord directs his Church in, through and with the Spirit, just as he promised.

When a Christian is baptized, he enters into the mystery of Christ: he is plunged, at one and the same time, into the death of Christ, his resurrection, and the outpouring of the Holy Spirit. Baptized in water, the symbol of regeneration, at the very same moment, he is baptized in the Holy Spirit, "the giver of life."

Baptism recreates for him the reality of a new Pentecost. We sometimes tend to read the Acts of the Apostles as we would an anthology relating occurrences of long ago. And so we see the Holy Spirit at work in the early communities, multiplying signs and wonders, lavishing gifts and charisms. But we relegate these happenings to the past—put them away in the archives. We find it hard to believe that these manifestations of the Spirit transcend time and space and remain ever present. We do not understand that the mystery of Pentecost continues, and that "God never takes back his gifts," as St. Paul says (Rom. 11, 29). There is a progressive logic and a continuity in God's ways with us. He does not advance in fits and starts nor go back on his tracks. We have in heaven a faithful witness, his ways unforeseeable, infinitely varied, and at times disturbing, nevertheless keeping always in the same constant direction. In this light of God's way of acting, it is evident that the episodes recorded in the pages of Scripture are not inconsequential, casual, leading nowhere. Through this history, set in Palestine and bearing its mark, faith sees a pattern of God's action that is valid for all time to come.

In fact, conversion, baptism, encounter with Jesus as Lord and Savior, receiving the Holy Spirit, are all parts of a unique whole, a complex reality. Tradition calls it "Christian initiation," "enlightenment," "entrance into a new life."

II. TODAY'S CHRISTIAN: IDEAL AND REALITY.

We have spent some time reflecting on the early Christians, though we know well enough that the ideal was never fully realized even by them and that the Holy Spirit is not bound to the past. We had to reflect in this way to be able to delineate the true nature of Christianity. But we have also to take a realistic look at Christianity as lived today, after twenty centuries during which the Gospel has been preached.

In our pilgrimage back to the sources, we saw that the early Christians were "converts"; persons who had received into their lives Jesus in all the profundity and mystery inherent in his person; that, moreover, they were open to his Spirit. I do not think that we can fail to be struck by the too frequent contrast between a Christian as outlined by Peter on the day following Pentecost and a Christian of today as the second millennium of the Christian era draws to a close. We have to open our eyes to this state of affairs if we hope to see the renewal of the Church become a reality: the Church is what its members are, no more, no less. The reform of the Church as a community depends upon those who make up this community: the "living stones" of the building are the Christians themselves. Let us try then to analyze as objectively as possible the situation as, in fact, it is. When we speak today of a Christian, about whom are we speaking?

AN ASSUMPTION THAT IS QUESTIONED TODAY.

During what we call the Christian centuries, it was commonly accepted that a Christian was, in the first place, someone who "practiced" his religion; that is, someone who could be recognized as such because he was present at Mass on Sundays and frequented the sacraments. No one questioned this assumption: a believer practices his faith, a non-believer does not. Faith was judged by a perceptible norm: namely, the practice of one's religion.

However, sociological research and observation have shown with brutal realism that our pastoral presupposition has to be examined anew. The wind of secularization has shaken the trees: some branches that looked green and luxuriant are broken; religious practice is diminishing everywhere, especially among the young. Everywhere we are confronted with a phenomenon which is a matter, not only of quantity, but of quality. What then, at the level of a faith as it is actually lived, is the "quality" of Christianity?

A recent study among the Catholics of France revealed some startling facts:

- of the 95% of the persons who want churches, the great majority never enter them;
- 88% have their children baptized, but
- more than half have no knowledge of Jesus Christ;
- two-thirds do not believe in the resurrection.

These statistics throw a harsh light on the true situation.

The French bishop from whose article I have taken these facts, analyzes them as follows:

"Will we, one day, decide to draw the logical conclusion from these studies or will we continue to give the sacraments to people who have no faith; to celebrate marriage or burial services, pretending that the bored, chatting congregation is really involved . . . 'Holy things for the holy.' Let the things of God be for those who believe in them. Let the sacraments be for those who have faith or who are sincerely wrestling with the problems presented by faith. We must rid ourselves, courageously, of all illusions. We held the second Vatican Council in the belief it was self-evident that Christians were essentially destined to be missionaries. But that presupposes that they are believers. The delay in the hoped-for renewal after Vatican II, the stampede of those who 'practice,' the proliferation of prophets who take from Christianity what suits them, the nostalgic cry for a 'tranquillizer' Christianity; all this can only be explained by the fact that, in our naïveté, we believed that the basic Christian message, the kerygma—'I believe in Jesus Christ, the Son of God, the Saviour'—was accepted and lived by everybody. In fact, this was true only of a few." [1]

If we compare the life of the early Christians with that of many today who are Christians in name only, the contrast is striking. And this poses the most radical problem of all in the renewal of the Church. The Council was a pastoral council; that is, it aimed at adapting the Church both within and without to the needs of the times. It presupposed as a basic hypothesis that the Church was made up of authentic Christians or, at least, those trying to be so. Now the facts compel us to question the validity of this presupposition. Again, when we speak of a Christian, of whom and of what are we speaking? This is a painful question because what we are asking is: "Do Christians in general today believe with a personal, dedicated and genuine faith?"

We have been occupied with revising the structures of the Church at many levels. This was necessary, and the enterprise is far from completion. However, today the very foundations of the faith are questioned. And yet the Church has meaning only in Christ. And Christ has meaning only if he is the Son of God. And God has meaning only if he is the living and personal God. But, alas, all this has become problematic!

Many people's faith is being shaken to its very foundations. They have to discover again the heart of the Christian message. We have "sacramentalized" on a large scale. We have not sufficiently "evangelized" and the extent of this deficiency can affect a whole continent, as, for instance, Latin America. But we see the same problem wherever Christians do not live by the logic of their faith.

Our left-wing, right-wing controversies pale beside this crisis. We are faced with the challenge of finding again what really makes a Christian. Our task is not to condemn our fellowmen, but without weakening, to uphold the Christian ideal. We must preach the authentic Gospel in its entirety and reveal to the world the Father, the Son and the Holy Spirit, as well as what God asks of those who bear witness to his name before the world.

We must help Christians to become continually more aware of their faith and live it on a more personal level. Many must be helped to exchange a sociological Christianity for a full and active life of faith. Christianity which we have inherited, which has its foundation mainly in the family and education, must mature into a Christianity of choice, based on a personal decision and embraced with full consciousness. As Tertullian has said: "Fiunt, non nascuntur christiani": "Christians become so, they are not born." [2]

A NEW KIND OF CHRISTIAN.

This, then, is the heart of the problem: how can we Christianize today such a vast number of nominal Christians? How can we evangelize a world which has become, to a large degree, post-Christian? What can we do, so that there may be a real flowering of a Christianity, freely chosen in which a Christian is recognized as someone who, fully aware of what is implied, is "converted" to Christ, who by an act of personal allegiance, ratifies the sacraments of his Christian initiation, baptism, confirmation and the eucharist; who moreover, opens himself, in expectant faith, to the action of the Holy Spirit and to his gifts, that he may be faithful to his supernatural calling.

This is at the heart of our pastoral problems: the glaring contrast between the nominal and the authentic Christian. And we must examine it closely. We are reproached not because we are Christians, but because we are not Christian enough. A Church which practices the faith does not suffice: it must be, above all, a Church which confesses that faith. We must proclaim Jesus Christ to the world of today and bear witness to our faith in him. "If anyone

declares himself for me in the presence of men, I will
declare myself for him in the presence of my Father in
heaven" (Mt. 10, 32). We need Christians who believe in
Jesus, the unique Son of the Father, who proclaim their
faith in the resurrection and in the active presence of his
Holy Spirit, and who translate that faith in every aspect of
their lives.

We need, in short, a Church composed of those who
want to belong, in whom the freedom of God's children is
so plain to see that the consequences of being a Christian
appear not as authoritarian injunctions imposed from
without under pain of mortal sin, but as imperatives felt
deep within us, springing up from a source that is the logic
of our faith.

Such a Church will be more and more that Church of
the diaspora of which Karl Rahner sometime ago drew a
prophetic picture and whose realization comes nearer
every day.

THE CHRISTIAN OF THE YEAR 2000.

Shortly after the close of Vatican II, Father Rahner, in
an address to the Catholic Students Association of
Freiburg University, gave a description of the Christian of
tomorrow, the Christian of the future. He portrayed this
Christian as a person totally surrendered to Christ, who
has freely chosen to live by his faith, one of a minority in
the world, but resolute, fraternal in his relations with his
fellow Christians and with all men:

"At that future date there will be Christian communities,
Catholic communities, all over the world though not evenly
distributed. Everywhere there will be little groups. Moreover
because mankind grows quicker than Christendom and because
men will not be Christians by custom and tradition, through
institutions and history, or because of the homogeneity of a

social milieu and public opinion, but—leaving out of account the sacred flame of parental example and the intimate atmosphere of home, family, and small gatherings—they will be Christians only because of their own act of personal faith decided upon after a difficult struggle and perpetually renewed. "Christians will all live in different degrees, in the diaspora of the gentiles. They will be the little flock of the Gospel . . . And so they will feel themselves as brothers to one another. Practically all will have surrendered their hearts and lives to Jesus Christ by a personal and deliberate decision. There will be few parasites for to be a Christian will offer no worldly advantage.

"The Church will be again a little flock of those sharing the same faith, the same hope, the same love. It will not pride itself on this, it will not think itself superior to earlier ages of the Church, but will obediently and thankfully accept its own age as is apportioned to it by the Lord and his Spirit . . ." [3]

But no matter what the future may bring, the Christian of today must live his faith with courage and conviction. Now more than ever he must draw his inspiration from those words which Peter spoke on the first Pentecost: he must experience conversion, and know once again a sense of sin; he must meet Jesus and rediscover his face and his word; he must accept the guidance of the Spirit, so that he may be led even where he may not want to go. In brief, he must be open to the future in a faith refilled with hope, because it is founded on the promise and the power of God.

III. TOWARDS GREATER CHRISTIAN AUTHENTICITY.

The contrast which we have just drawn between these two types of Christians forces us to a serious examination of conscience: the religious future of generations will depend on its conclusions.

A RADICAL CHANGE.

First of all, we must look the situation squarely in the face. Whether we like it or not, we must accept the fact that tomorrow's Christian will be less and less a Christian by heredity, someone situated in and upheld by a solid Christian family tradition. Each will have to choose for himself, in full clarity and freedom, whether he wants to have his life animated by Jesus Christ or not. No adult will be able to be a Christian by proxy: the decision will be in his hands and will depend, largely, on the kind of Christianity he is being offered and which he sees being lived. He will need doctrine, and living examples.

It is difficult to realize how the present situation differs from that of the early Christians; now we baptize children rather than adults. The first Christians were already adults, called to be converted, to accept the word of God with a complete freedom which totally transformed their way of life and could lead them even to martyrdom.

Little by little the situation changed and the Church baptized infants. One breathed and lived in the atmosphere of a Christian home, even in a society that professed to be Christian: religion was taken for granted. Pastoral activity was focused on maintaining a Christian atmosphere. Nowadays, in a great number of countries, all that is past.

As a consequence, there are new questions to answer, beginning with that of infant baptism itself and the choice the young adult will have to make. I would like to reflect on our responsibilities in this respect. First of all: should we continue to baptize children or should we leave that to the decision of each young adult?

I. INFANT BAPTISM: A QUESTION.

The question of infant baptism springs naturally to the mind the moment one takes baptism seriously. If, in the light of all that we have said, baptism was for the most part an adult decision to opt for Jesus and acknowledge him as Lord, then would it not seem logical to defer this sacrament until a person was capable of encountering Jesus and accepting his Spirit and his gospel?

Respecting traditions.

Nonetheless, the Church has always firmly held—with good reason—to the tradition of infant baptism, provided of course, the parents guaranteed a minimum of Christian formation for their child. This condition is supremely important, if baptism is not to be just a conventional ceremony, devoid of real meaning. The Church cannot agree to the de-sacralization of baptism nor to lending itself to a ceremony which, in the eyes of certain parents, is only a social convention: a kind of blessing or "charm" devoid of religious content. The priest who is to baptize a child must make the consequences of this act clear, especially if the parents are non-practicing Christians, or even non-believers. It may indeed be painful for the priest to take this line. When the case arises he will need exceptional discernment, to see if this is the time to apply the words of Jesus not to extinguish the smoking flax; or if he must insist upon the respect due to baptism as a gift of God which commits one's life to Christ in a solemn covenant.

The retaining of infant baptism.

But the priest may also meet with the opposite situation: sincere Christian parents wish to defer baptism, considering it would be better for the child to decide for himself when he reaches maturity. Can a priest approve of such a position?

I would like to say here, briefly, why Christian parents should choose to have their child baptized despite the question they raise of future liberty. Let us establish this, first by reflecting from the point of view of the parents themselves and then, at a deeper level, from the point of view of God who comes to meet the child at this beginning of his life.

If we consider first, the point of view of parental responsibility, we see that, naturally, parents must assume responsibilities on behalf of their children. They have brought the child into the world, and immediately they are faced with making decisions for him as to what is for his good. They want to give him, from the first moment of his life, all their tender care, all the attention, which their own experience has taught them will be beneficial for him, even when this involves making certain decisions without consulting him. Their watchful and unfaltering love surrounds the child constantly. This is the beauty of their love, that they are not waiting for a recompense. Without being aware of it, they are following the way in which God loves us: he first loves us, without awaiting our initiative or gratitude.

Jesus said the same of our Christian vocation: "You did not choose me, I chose you" (Jn. 15, 16). It is a response to this choice, this initial love of God for us. Should we not follow this principle when it comes to baptism? From the beginning of the child's life God wishes to give the best of himself, his inner life: this is the meaning of baptism. Baptism introduces the child into divine intimacy, joins him to the mystery of the death and resurrection of the Lord himself, opens him to the grace of the Holy Spirit. These are all real riches even if at the beginning the child is unaware of this. It is important that an awareness of these realities should grow slowly, in the process of a Christian life nourished by the Eucharist. To postpone baptism is to deprive the child of this growth of grace within him. It is to take away from the young person in the name of freedom, what will be, at the moment of a decisive choice an inestimable treasure that is the experience of living the Christian life. By depriving the child of this experience, he, whether one wishes it or not, is being "conditioned" and this lacuna will be a powerful factor in his making a choice: he cannot with impunity breathe a rarefied religious atmosphere at home and a hostile atmosphere outside. The liberty of the child is not safeguarded by denying him an experience which can help motivate his free choice at the deepest level.

For the same reasons, I think we should continue to confer confirmation, the complement of baptism, during a person's earlier years. The child receives this sacrament, too, to some degree, in virtue of the parents' faith and the same overall significance. He must ratify this as an adult, but in the meantime, the grace of the sacrament can operate within him to the degree of his growing fidelity.

2. A NECESSARY RE-ASSESSMENT.

If we should maintain the practice of infant baptism, we should also assume new responsibilities in relation to the young adult, who is called upon to ratify the obligations implied in the sacraments of Christian initiation which he received. One cannot, however, become a Christian automatically. For each person there is a unique road to bring him to full Christian maturity. In one form or another every young person will be challenged by the demands contained in Peter's words at the conclusion of his address: "Repent, and every one of you must be baptized in the name of Jesus Christ for the forgiveness of your sins, and you will receive the gift of the Holy Spirit" (Acts 2, 38). To become truly a Christian one must agree, in full freedom, to be converted, to repent and turn to Christ, and accept his Holy Spirit. We cannot escape these obligations.

The primary duty of Christians today is to show forth in themselves what it means to be "converted" and "filled with the Holy Spirit." This is the specific mission of modern Christians who try to respond to the demands of the Gospel and to share their faith in the midst of the world in which they live. Thanks be to God, there are many such Christians still. And although those who are only "sociological" Christians do not allow us to guess what true Christianity means, these others give an idea of the attraction it holds. However, in spite of their good will and fruitful efforts, their influence is stifled by the surrounding non-Christian atmosphere; their light can hardly pierce the darkness. To overcome the obstacles confronting them and to encourage the "semi-Christians" who follow in their wake, they need an increase of power, a heightening of spiritual energy: they need the Holy Spirit.

The Council, which was itself, according to John XXIII, an inspiration of the Holy Spirit, invites us to discover afresh the role of the Spirit who "orders all things sweetly." Our liturgical reform has placed at the heart of each Eucharist an appeal for his help. The manifestation of the gifts of the Spirit, which we see burgeoning everywhere are like the buds that tell us spring has come. All these heavenly signs are from God calling us to become more deeply aware of who we are as Christians, to be converted to the Lord and given over to the action of his Spirit. Christians who are truly and increasingly "the faithful," will be the leaven that makes the dough rise.

The need for sound teaching.

Among these Christians is a group who are especially responsible for the future: men and women who are called to a teaching mission in the Church. Theirs, in a unique way, is the responsibility of showing in their lives, to the generations of today and tomorrow, what it means to be a Christian.

Bishops, theologians, priests, committed Christians, each with their own charisms and at their particular level, must embody in their lives this concept of being "converted" and "filled with the Holy Spirit." Then, they will be able to pass on to others the real teaching of the Master. Young people more than ever before are sensitive to what a person lives, to what a person does and ask not for words but for a concrete demonstration of what we hold true. They often say to us: "I can't hear what you're saying because you're talking too loud." We must be able to read the Scriptures with them at their pace and show them that between the Christianity of yesterday and that of today there is no break in continuity.

QUESTIONS AND INTERROGATIONS.

And now a clear-sighted examination of conscience! I have to examine myself, ask some direct questions: "Am I really converted? Do I honestly have my whole soul turned toward the Lord in a true *metanoia?* Am I content with keeping clear of overt sin and calling this conversion, while at the same time clinging to a wisdom that is all my own, my own ideas, my prudence, my notions of how things should be? Have I really accepted Jesus as my Lord in all the concrete events of my life? Is he truly in my personal experience, the way, the truth, the life? Yes, in how broad a sense can I use the word 'life'? Can I say with St. Paul, 'Now it is not I who live, it is Christ who lives in me' (Gal. 2, 20)?" Finally, dare I simply say: "I believe, and I am ready to accept in my life all the consequences?"

These questions can be put another way. I can ask myself whether or not I have agreed to be "christianized" by Christ, "spiritualized" by his Spirit, and whether I really expect the Spirit to manifest his gifts in me today, so that I can preach Christ in the twentieth century. On the day of my episcopal ordination, the bishop who ordained me confided to me the mission of being a shepherd in God's Church, in the power of signs and wonders. Did I and do I believe that the Lord asks me to surrender to the powerful action of the Holy Spirit as he did?

The Christian of tomorrow will not be able to face the future if we have not passed on to him a Christianity full of hope. We must give to him a faith which is strong and exhilarating: grafted on to the power of the Holy Spirit, protected under the shadow of his wings, performing "signs and wonders" which attest that we too live in that burgeoning of new life which is Pentecost.

We should consider again the Gospel scene where Jesus applies to himself the prophecy of Isaiah, telling how the Holy Spirit came upon him before he announced the good news to the world: "The Spirit of the Lord has been given to me, for he has anointed me . . . to bring the good news to the poor . . ." (Lk. 4, 18). We must listen again to the order that Jesus gave to his disciples before sending them forth to overcome the world: "Stay in the city then, until you are clothed with the power from on high" (Lk. 24, 49). We ought to meditate once again the Acts of the Apostles —the scenes evoked provide a catechism in picture—and learn what Christianity really is. We see Peter standing before the crowd, calmly telling them that the prophecy of Joel has been accomplished before their eyes: "In the days to come, I will pour out my Spirit on all mankind. Their sons and daughters shall prophesy . . . Even on my slaves, men and women, in those days I will pour out my Spirit. I will display portents in heaven above and signs on earth below" (Acts 2, 17–19). Then Peter spoke of Jesus and recalled: "Jesus the Nazarene was a man commended to you by God by the miracles and portents and signs that

God worked through him when he was among you, as you all know" (Acts 2, 22). Christianity was indeed being *lived*.

In the light of these inspired texts, we ought to present a very different picture of a "normal" Christian, exorcising our fears in the face of what could appear as "exaggerations" of the Holy Spirit. It is time we change our vocabulary and stop calling "prudence" what is fear, and "wisdom" what is timidity, when faced with implementing the Gospel.

If we do this, we can define our Christian identity, proclaim it in "deed and in truth" and pass it on, unimpaired, to those who replace us tomorrow.

The Holy Spirit
and New Communities

Faith will be fraternal,
that is, lived in community,
or it will not exist at all.
P. Liégé

What the Church needs today, more than
new institutions or programs,
are vital Christian communities.[1]
S. Clark

I. THE FIRST IMAGE OF THE CHURCH:
A CHRISTIAN BROTHERHOOD.

In our journey back to the sources of Christianity, we saw
what characterizes an authentic Christian: he is converted;
that is he has turned to Jesus with all his heart, he has
acknowledged him as Lord and Saviour, and he is open to
the Holy Spirit.

Now we must reflect on the nature of the early Christian
communities. Though twenty centuries separate us, and
our socio-cultural context is completely different, we must
still look to them for the essential elements of Christian
community life: we cannot afford to be cut off from our
past. And at the same time, the very contrast brings us to
examine our conscience.

Today, the word "Church" evokes, at first sight, the image of a highly organized society extending over all continents and regulating the life of over 500 million people by means of universal laws promulgated by the Pope. We think of an "institution" along with other "institutions," of which we speak in terms of politics or sociology; in the same breath we speak of civil, military, and also ecclesiastical authorities. We often talk of the crisis in the Church today as if the Church were an absolute monarchy threatened by the opposing currents of democracy. But this is to look through the wrong end of the telescope: it distorts the Church and moves it further from us instead of bringing it closer.

It is certainly true that, since the Church exists for men and women in the world, it has also the dimension of a society or institution. But in its depths the Church is first and foremost a community of persons who acknowledge Jesus of Nazareth, who died and rose from the dead, as Savior of all mankind, as Lord and unique Son of the Father. And in him they aim at living the exigencies of their faith, between themselves and with their fellowmen.

The Church has concrete existence only where believers assemble to hear the Word, to pray, to celebrate the Last Supper and to dedicate themselves to a life of faith and love that, of its very nature, is personal and communal.

Father Louis Bouyer writes: "At the outset, the Church did not exist as a worldwide organization of cult, evangelization and Christian charity. Rather, at the beginning, it was, necessarily, a local gathering of communities made up of believers who met to celebrate the Eucharist."[2]

The acts of the Apostles show us a community of Christians, disciples of Jesus, closely bound to one another, sometimes to the point of sharing all they had. The first Christians, those three thousand converts, who on the morning of Pentecost listened to the words of Peter and the Apostles, appear in the Acts as:

An apostolic community, "faithful to the teaching of the apostles";

A brotherly community, sustained by frequent contacts and frequent meetings;

A eucharistic community, celebrating the memorial of the Lord, "until he comes";

A prayer community, first in the temple, and then more and more, "in their houses." [3]

Such were the dominant traits by which the Church was recognized at the beginning. The warmth of mutual love was the mark of their credibility. People used to say: "Look, how they love one another!" They were struck by the joy of these Christians, their simplicity of heart, their genuine affection. We would say today that their actions were consistent with their teaching; they were trying to live in accordance with a profound, simple logic: "If a man does not love the brother he can see, he cannot love God whom he has never seen" (1 Jn. 4, 20).

The bond uniting them had nothing to do with temperamental affinity or romantic enthusiasm. The communion, or community—the *koinonia*—experienced internal tensions that had to be overcome in the power of the mystery which had done away with the differences between master and slave, male and female, Jew and Greek.

Nor was this community held together by a common ideology or a detailed code of life. Born of the encounter with Someone, it could think of itself only in terms of a faith that confessed that Someone.

The group was *koinonia* because first of all it experienced a living communion with the risen Jesus, and then with one another, proclaiming that Jesus was Lord.

It was *martyrion* because it bore witness to its Lord even to the point of martyrdom.

The community was also *diakonia* because it was based on mutual service, particularly the care of brethren in need. We have only to think how the Christians shared their possessions, or of Paul's collections for the poor of Jerusalem. In this perspective, all the varied ministries, the *diakoniai*, were looked upon as service rendered to the community.

The first pastoral services had their origin in this early community. They were never conceived of as merely emanations of the group: the Lord, at the beginning, had provided his Church with an apostolic ministry which was linked to him in a particular way. However, these services were at the very heart of this newly born community.

The Second Vatican Council accentuated the fundamentally fraternal aspect of the Church by calling it, in the second chapter of *Lumen Gentium*, the People of God— People comprising all the baptized, People who know one another as brothers and sisters. In this, Vatican II was echoing the tradition about which we learn in the Acts of the Apostles, which described the decision of the "Council of Jerusalem" as taken in common by "The apostles, the elders, and the whole assembly," and transmitted to the Christians of Antioch, Syria and Cilicia as coming from the entire community: "It is the decision of the Holy Spirit and our decision, to lay no further burden upon you beyond the essentials" (Acts 15, 28).

Throughout the first three centuries, the Christians lived a communal life as a matter of course. The word "Church" meant assembly, and another word for assembly was "brotherhood," as the letter of Peter reminds us.[4] Particular churches addressed letters to other local churches, and bishops sent messages to churches other than their own. Paul's letter to the Romans, for example, is not an isolated case. At the beginning of the second century, St. Ignatius of Antioch addressed seven letters to local churches, only one of which was to his own. Christianity was lived together and what pertained to one was the concern of all. Between the third and sixth centuries, however, there was an historic process of evolution. This exaggerated the juridical and institutional aspects of the Church, as well as the distinction between clergy and laity, which finally resulted in there being two classes of persons within the Church.

This is not, of course, to deny that hierarchy and priestly ministry are specific realities; their particular role is acknowledged to be the very heart of a fraternal community. Hence, the strongly pastoral character of religious authority. It was not without reason that the Church adopted the image of shepherd to designate its leaders. Not only is this in keeping with the Gospel which shows Jesus as the Good Shepherd, but it corresponds to the living experience of the community of the faithful. There is a deep vision of Church in St. Peter's advice to his fellow elders: "Be the shepherd of the flock of God that is entrusted to you. . . . be an example the whole flock can follow. When the chief shepherd appears you will be given the crown of unfading glory" (1 Pt. 5, 1–4). The role of a shepherd is not primarily to rule or preside over a flock but to gather and keep it together, make of it a unity.

II. CHRISTIANITY IS COMMUNAL.

The Church began its life as the sum total of small Christian communities dispersed here and there in the Roman world, where they fulfilled the role assigned by the Lord to be the salt of the earth and leaven in the dough. Through a deep interior drive, the power of the Holy Spirit at work, the Church step by step took shape. We are now discovering that the future Church will be the Church of the diaspora—an added reason why we must draw inspiration from our origins. I am convinced more than ever that the future of the Church will be conditioned by the strength and quality of its communal life. The Church will be what the Christian communities are, as they grow and develop into the mystical Body of Christ.

Christianity and individualism are exclusive. Living the Christian life means essentially to allow Christ to become the common life shared by Christians. It is to leave the Spirit free to build the Church in us in the diversity and convergence of his complementary gifts. Is it not the purpose of these gifts that they be a manifestation of the Spirit for the common good? The fundamental guarantee of their authenticity is found in the mutual control, internal evaluation and communal discernment which enriches the community and harmonizes divergencies. It has been said: "We have to be many to be intelligent". We can also say, we have to be many to be Christian. Besides, the Lord said: "Where two or three meet in my name, I shall be there with them" (Mt. 18, 20). This promise has its roots within the Trinity.

To make more real the plurality contained in the Trinity a well known theologian, Heribert Muehlen, speaks of the Father as the "I," the Son as the "You," and the Holy Spirit as the "We" of the Trinity. In that light we could say that "One has to be 'many' to be God." This is the transcendent plural unity given to us by Jesus as the exemplar of our life together. Every Christian is a communal being.

If no man is an island, this applies even more to someone who is baptized. Even the Pope cannot isolate himself. "The Pope has need of brothers," Patriarch Athenagoras said. That this special presence of Jesus can be realized we need a minimal community of two or three. It is "together" we must live the Christian life. Unless my brothers and sisters are close to me, how can I share spiritual bread? How else can each of us put our charisms at the service of all? The Church is not an abstraction: before being a 'world'-church, the Church was the Church of Corinth, the Church of Ephesus, the Church of Rome. The more we are aware of the Church as a specific community, the more real and alive it becomes.

COMMUNITY LIFE AS A PRESENT NEED.

Christianity is essentially communal. This is true of every time and place. Today, however, a believer must find again community life not only to live his faith but to survive as a Christian in a world growing more and more estranged from Christianity. It is always hard to swim against the current; we are swept along despite ourselves —for a man is more the son of his time than he is the son of his father. Today we are in extreme danger of being moulded to a pattern by a society which wants to impose its own image, its own criteria which admit of no discussion. If we have made progress in many spheres, in others we are in reverse. We need only recall the lowering of standards in public morality, the extent of violence and the increase in crime. Christians breathe this air, they cannot live their faith in some hermetically sealed ghetto, protected from every contagion.

Steve Clark has written:

"A Christian must have an environment in his life in which Christianity is openly accepted, talked about, and lived if he is going to be able to live a very vital Christian life. If he does not have this, his whole life as a Christian will be weak and might even die away. Yet fewer and fewer Catholics are finding such an environment . . . When society as a whole cannot be expected to accept Christianity, then it is necessary to form communities within society to make Christian life possible . . . Because they had been taught to identify 'what was right' in matters of religion with 'what was accepted by society as a whole,' most people began to weaken in their Christian conviction and their Christian living when they saw that Christianity was not being accepted by society as a whole the way it had been."[5]

WHAT IS A BASIC CHRISTIAN COMMUNITY?

More than ever, then, we feel the need to create authentic Christian communities but a label such as "basic community" [6] even in a Christian context, covers realities which are very different.

Max Delespesse, a Belgian priest, and currently director of the *Centre Communautaire International* in Brussels, has remarked that the term "basic community" is often applied to groups whose members are united not by common life but by common activities. These can have their *raison d'être*, but when speaking here of Christian communities, we mean people sharing a common life from which their activities spring. There are different degrees of this living together, but it is not to our purpose to analyze these here. In a Christian context, even having a life in common does not constitute a Christian community. A community is only authentically Christian in relation to Jesus Christ whom its members accept explicitly and strive to follow as Master, as Savior, as Lord. A community is only truly Christian if it has answered the call of Jesus to be guided by his Spirit. Dietrich Bonhoeffer draws attention to this fundamental point when he writes:

"In Christian brotherhood everything depends upon its being clear right from the beginning; first, that Christian brotherhood is not a human ideal, but a divine reality; secondly, that Christian brotherhood is a spiritual and not a psychic reality. Innumerable times whole Christian communities have come to nothing because they had a false idea of the Church." [7]

This reflection has not lost its relevance. Looking through a periodical, I came across this definition of a basic community: "A basic community is not so much concerned with proclaiming Jesus Christ as questioning itself about Jesus and living out faith as a constant search. Such communities try to integrate their political action

and their Christian faith." Every word here needs clarifica-
tion. A community, if it is Christian in the exact and full
sense of the term, cannot but proclaim Jesus Christ: "Woe
to me if I do not preach the Gospel!" (1 Cor. 9, 16). Paul's
words do not mean preaching without discernment or tact.
There are many ways to "proclaim" Jesus Christ. But a
Christian must have an earnest desire to bring the Gospel
to every man despite all obstacles and resistance.

When one writes: "A community questioning itself
about Jesus and living out faith as a constant search,"
what does this mean? Yes, we can question ourselves
about Jesus and seek to understand him better, but this
questioning must be rooted in faith and evolve in it; this is
the precise aim of theology. The alternative—and it is a
quite different hypothesis—is to question the very foundation of faith itself.

One is happy to see people searching together the
meaning of faith and of Christianity. But such groups are
not yet Christian communities: one has to respect the
significance of words. One can discuss the best ways of
expressing a mystery but a Christian is one who adheres to
the very mystery of the divinity and resurrection of Jesus.

At the basis of every Christian community, there is the
common acceptance of Jesus and his message. To the
question, "What is a Christian?" we answer too often that
he is someone upright and just, loving, morally sensitive,
aware of his responsibility to society. But many non-Christians possess all these qualities, sometimes to a greater
degree than we ourselves. Well, then? The uniqueness of
Christianity, that which makes it what it really is, is not a
complex of principles and values: it is Jesus Christ. The
meaning of his life, his death, his resurrection, and his
living presence among us by his Spirit—these are the
essence of Christianity.

If Christ is a vague name standing for love of humanity
and if one reduces the Gospel to a social humanism, then

the name of Jesus differs little from that of any great prophet of the human race. It is useless to talk about the renewal of the Church, if this renewal is not first and foremost a fresh discovery, of all that is implied in an intimate and personal relationship between Jesus Christ and the believer. We must therefore first be clear as to what baptism in Christ means, if we want to live by the logic implicit in it.

Jesus Christ is the cornerstone, the foundation of every Christian community. If such a community is to live and to continue to live, it must have a justification for doing so. This justification is Christ. Nothing can take his place. It is he who gives life to the community by his Holy Spirit. Without him, there can be a meeting between persons, but no true communion.

Once again, no one has better expressed than Dietrich Bonhoeffer, the role of the Holy Spirit in uniting us with one another. This Lutheran theologian put to death by the Nazis continues to be one of the thinkers most popular among the young. His letters written in prison are especially quoted, though they do not do justice to the whole range of his work. The following, taken from his book "On the True Nature of the Church," recalls that, since Pentecost, it is always the Spirit who forms a "gathering," that is a "Church."

"A gathering of men, he writes, come together. The Spirit comes upon the assembled gathering. They are all one in 'having the same wind,' waiting for the Spirit because of Jesus' promise (Acts 1). First the gathering, then the Spirit comes. The gathering is not already the Church. It only becomes the Church through the Spirit. But the Spirit comes on those who are already gathered together. Man can do nothing for his salvation, but he can go to the Church; the promise of the Spirit is given to the individual only in so far as he is a member of a community, gathered together. Now the entirely new thing happens: the Spirit comes. The coming of the Spirit and the founding of the

Church is a visible event, and not an incorporeal concept. The Spirit makes a place for himself in the world by coming with visible signs. The community is immediately placed visibly before everyone else; it is given up to their judgment. The founding of the Church is no hidden thing, 'done in a corner'; it is a visible designation of all those who have been called. The Spirit exposes his community to the world. It immediately becomes 'the city on the hill, which cannot be hid.' The Spirit comes in the Word, not in stuttering and stammering, but in words that can be understood by all. That is the meaning of the miracle of tongues: it is a language understood by all. It is the unitive Word. It is a Word which makes man responsible. The Spirit says the one word that everyone understands.

"By becoming visible, the Church is immediately subjected to the judgment of the world. The visible phenomenon of the Spirit is thus nothing unequivocal in the world. Where the Spirit is, the world sees drunkenness and folly. But it is precisely the world's mockery that will again and again be the sign that the Church is on the right road; it is a clearer sign than the world's applause. Where the Church retreats into invisibility, it despises the reality of the Spirit." [8]

III. PARISH AND COMMUNITY.

The Holy Spirit, the life-giving breath of the Church, must penetrate not only the Church as a whole but all its parts. As we have already said, spiritual renewal can only normally come to maturity if it takes root in the real day to day life of believers who are able to live in a Christian atmosphere. The Christian is more conditioned by the milieu in which he lives than he is by the structures within which his milieu is enclosed. True Christian communities are the starting point for a Christianity that is alive; they form the tissue of the organism which is the Church.

This brings us to a delicate question: relationship between these basic communities and the unity of the parish which is the structural foundation of the Church.

CHRISTIAN COMMUNITY AND PARISH STRUCTURE.

There is no need to trace the history of the parish as we know it today: almost everywhere the parish is the basic structure of the Church. So long as the parish more or less fitted into the life of a Christian, there was no problem; the parish was the centre of Christian life. The phenomenon of urban expansion, modern life, increased mobility, secularization, pluralism in society upset the balance. Our parishes in cities and towns are out of all proportion. Hence, for the priest and the faithful, the difficulty of forming the genuine personal relationships that are indispensable to every living community. Let us read again, by way of contrast, the ending of St. Paul's letter to the Romans. What warmth there is!

"I commend to you our Sister Phoebe, a deaconess of the Church at Cenchreae. Give her, in union with the Lord, a welcome worthy of saints, and help her with anything she needs: she has looked after a great many people, myself included.
My greetings to Prisca and Aquila, my fellow workers in Christ Jesus, who risked their lives for me. I am not the only one to owe them a debt of gratitude. So do all the Gentile Churches.
Greetings also to the Church that meets at their house.
Greetings to my dear Epaenetus, the first person in the province of Asia to give himself to Christ.
Greetings to Mary who has worn herself out working for you.
Greetings to Andronicus and Junias, my kinsmen who were with me in prison, they are well known among the apostles and became Christians before I did.
Greetings to Ampliatus, dear to me in the Lord.
Greetings to Urban, our fellow worker in Christ and my beloved Stachys.
Greetings to Apelles who proved his devotion to Christ.
Greetings to everyone who belongs to the household of Aristobulus.
Greetings to Herodion, my kinsmen, and those of the household of Narcissus who belong to the Lord.

Greetings to Tryphaena and Tryphosa, who work hard in the service of the Lord; to my friend Persis who has done so much for the Lord; to Rufus, the chosen servant of the Lord, and to his mother who has also been a mother to me.

Greetings to Asyncritus, Phlegon, Hermes, Patrobas, Hermes, and all the brothers who are with them.

Greetings to Philologus and Julia, Nereus and his sister, and Olympas and all the God's people who are with them.

Greet each other with a holy kiss. All the Churches of Christ send you greetings" (Rom. 16, 1–16).

Great efforts are being expended, despite the anonymity of our towns, to make parishes alive and to concentrate on the community aspect. In the post-Conciliar Church, this has been particularly noticeable in the area of liturgy. If we compare our celebrations of the Eucharist today with those of a few years ago, we cannot fail to recognize that, in general, there has been a considerable degree of renewal. We have become once again, a gathering of Christians praying together, listening together, to the word of God and aware that the Eucharist must lead up to communion and be continued in acts of friendliness at every level. We have not reached the ideal, but we are on the right road.

Nevertheless, if we look closely at those who come together in our churches on Sunday, we must admit that they do not give the impression of a truly living fellowship. In the same Sunday congregation we regularly find Christians of very different types, from the deeply committed and fervent, to those who are there from force of habit. We do not intend to judge or classify the density of Christian vitality in individual cases: this is the secret of God. We are conditioned to count as "Christians" those who frequent the sacraments even to some degrees: we rarely try to determine whether or not these same people put their faith into practice at other levels. There are many who are Christians on the surface. Authentic Christians

are more rare. This being so, it is important to plan
pastoral measures that will reach these different levels
from the sociological Christians to those who are fully
committed to their faith. We will have to see that both
these spheres of pastoral activity converge.

It is possible to have many different kinds of relationships between the existing parish structure and the basic
communities. These will depend largely upon circumstances and the persons involved. There is no need to
choose one kind of community life rather than another,
since both types are necessary for the life of the Church at
this moment. What is important is that there be harmony
between their respective activities and growth. But it is
essential that the basic communities be not marginal in
relation to the bishop, the vital center of the local ecclesial
community.

In a given parish the solution can be to let each
community develop along its own lines, while maintaining
a minimum of contact with the parish. There is some
advantage in this fundamental unity amid marked plurality. It can happen that in a given parish a living
community, may be instrumental in animating the whole
parish and bring it the spiritual inspiration often so badly
needed. Every one agrees there are many such. Obviously
efforts of that kind will not take place without some
tension and conflict. This suffering arising out of mutual
misunderstanding can be redemptive suffering for the
world.

As to Charismatic Renewal groups, Kevin Ranaghan
describes their possible integration in the parish:

"We must also try to integrate our prayer groups and communities into parish and diocesan life. There is no one model for this
work. Charismatic prayer groups and communities assume a
variety of styles as do parishes and dioceses. In some places, the
Charismatic Renewal may become the pastoral strategy for the
renewal of the parish; elsewhere, the prayer group may be

simply an approved activity within the parish. In some cities, large charismatic associations or covenant communities drawing people from many parishes will need to have a liaison with the bishop and his diocesan staff. In some cities the community may look much like a new religious congregation; in others, it will take the form of a new diocesan-wide confraternity." [9]

The most striking example known to me of a fully successful integration of institution and charism at the parish level is that of the Episcopalian parish of the Church of the Redeemer in Eastwood, a poor section of Houston, Texas. The story of this parish has been told by its founder Graham Pulkingham in *Gathered for Power*; and in greater detail by Michael Harper in *A New Way of Living*.[10] Having actually witnessed this experience on the spot, I can only confirm what is said in these books.

The pastor and four of his friends, animated by a deep charismatic spirituality, succeeded, by a gradual osmosis, in winning over other members of the parish to their vision of renewal. Gradually, in the power of the Spirit, these formed a community which lives a kind of community life described in the Acts of the Apostles, even sharing their possessions.

At this moment, there are about thirty persons, men and women, engaged full time in the various ministries of the parish and even beyond, which they sum up under the fivefold division of apostle, prophet, evangelist, shepherd, teacher. Grouped around this core is a community of about five hundred persons, living in forty households. These Christians, who belong to the parish consecrate a considerable part of their time to ministering to the various spiritual, moral and material needs of the neighborhood. It is a marvelous example of a Christianity lived in all its social implications, within a climate of deep prayer, personal as well as communal and liturgical. This example has been followed. Many other parishes have begun similar communal life patterns, especially among Roman Catholics as for instance John Randall, P.P., of St. Patrick's parish, Providence, Rhode Island, who tells of his experience in a small book: *In God's Providence: the Birth of a Charismatic Parish.*[11]

To conclude this section, it is worthwhile to read these lines of Louis Rétif who believes that if the parish and community were complementary, great advantages would ensue.

Among them he sees:

> "More humane units, created by life situations,
> liturgy becoming again a festive celebration;
> ministries redistributed among clergy and laity;
> a new awakening of prophecy in the Church;
> a better integration of the priest in the community."

All this, under the condition that these groups would have the time to grow and the right to make mistakes, he concludes this way:

> "Essentially, the question here is one of making anew the very fabric of Christian life. Only communities of human proportions, rooted in life and present there where men live, struggle and hope; only communities and apostolic groups engaged in truly prophetic initiatives, inspired by a liberty conferred by the Spirit, and yet in communion with the Church can give new life to the whole Body." [12]

IV. THE PROPHETIC ROLE OF VITAL CHRISTIAN COMMUNITIES.

Vatican II called the Church the "sacrament of the world's unity." This means that the Church is a sign and a promise for a world which longs for unity, peace and full human development. To fulfill this mission, the Church must be able to offer, as it were, pilot projects which are a prefiguration of the kind of human community for which the world is searching so painfully. The Church must be able to show, in miniature, what the world can become if men accept Jesus as the Savior of the world, the key to its problems. I use the word "key" advisedly, in the sense that at the very root of the world's suffering are hatred, jealousy, personal and collective egoism, a "non-love" under many forms; in short, what we Christians call sin. Jesus alone can reach and move the depths of the heart, and as a consequence change man-made structures. Only an open acceptance of Jesus as the Way, the Truth and the Life can radically get to the heart of our problems and only his Church possesses the power that can renew not only the face of the Church but also that of the whole earth. Strange talk to our Christian ears, you will say, when our faith is weak, our hope wavering. But to be a Christian is to believe in this with all one's being: neither more nor less.

Christians can help the world to progress toward a new humanity in offering to mankind, on a reduced human scale, by way of pilot experiences, the image of genuine brotherhood. In seeing Christians live their faith, the world should be shocked into asking: "What is the secret of this mutual love, this serenity, this forgetfulness of self?" The name of Jesus Christ would stand out as never before, because in his followers, a radiance and transparency would reveal his life within theirs. This is the sign of credibility given by Jesus himself; the only effective *apologia.* Christian life has a prophetic value in the world. As J. J. von Allmen has said: "A baptized person is a sign of promise for all men, a eucharist is a promise for every meal; and the Church is a promise for all human society."

We tend to overlook the role of the community as that of an intermediary, between the Christian and world. We should live Christianity "at home" before exporting it. We should study more closely the relations between Christians in the Scriptures. Love between brothers has a priority. St. Paul says: "While we have the chance, we must do good to all, and especially to our brothers in the faith" (Gal. 6, 10). Let us not be like those people who are "impossible" in their own homes but charming towards strangers. Charity begins at home and spreads from there to those outside. We need to reach the world step by step and by gradual stages. To a large degree, the renewal of the Church will begin when Christian communities become places of light and warmth for those around them.

From a human point of view, it might seem paradoxical to make the future of the Church dependent upon small Christian communities which, no matter how fervent, are but a drop in the ocean. This is true. But if we consider the spiritual energy released by every group which allows Christ to fill it with the life of his Holy Spirit, then the perspective changes, for we are putting ourselves in the strength and power of God. The "little" flock of the Gospel is the symbol of the Christian minority, that minority which Dom Helder Camara likes to call the "Abraham" minority. It is minorities, in fact, which change the world.

John Henry Newman, in his essay "On the Present Position of Catholics in England," has shown this law of salvation history: that it is the apparently weak that bring force to the world.

"It is not giants who do most . . . Moses was one, Elias was one, David was one, Paul was one, Athanasius was one, Leo was one. Grace ever works by few, it is the keen vision, the intense conviction, the indomitable resolve of the few; it is the blood of the martyrs, it is the prayer of the saint, it is the hero's deed, it is the momentary crisis, it is the concentrated energy of a word or a look, which is the instrument of heaven. Fear not, little flock, for He is mighty who is in the midst of you, and He will do for you great things." [13]

V. TWO EXAMPLES OF NEW
COMMUNAL EXPERIENCES.

The Church is experiencing the stirrings of the Holy Spirit
in many parts of the world. To conclude this chapter
about new communities, I would like to give two examples
of communal life inspired by the Holy Spirit in our time.
One is based on a new manner of living in fraternal love;
the other on the renewal of a love relationship between
husband and wife. I choose these two examples because I
have been able to observe them closely since the closing of
the Council. Each of these experiences holds out, I believe,
rich hope for the future.

THE COMMUNAL LIFE OF THE FOCOLARINI.

This collective form of living the Gospel life began in
Trent, in northern Italy in 1943. It comes to us, then, from
the country of St. Francis and St. Clare, and there are in
the movement certain characteristics that call to mind the
early Franciscans, the *fioretti* included. God's instrument
was a woman, Chiara Lubich. In the middle of the war,
when bombs were falling Chiara used to read aloud
passages of the Gospel to console people huddling for
refuge in the shelters. She also put the Gospel into practice
in daily acts of love. Some young women joined her. The
local people, sympathetically disposed, called them "focol-
arine" because they found in them the light and warmth of
Christ: the official name is now *Opera di Maria*.[14] Very
soon, other Christians, men and women, married and
single, laity and priests, attracted by their spirituality
began to join them, making ever-widening concentric
circles around the small groups, whose members take the
three vows of poverty, chastity and obedience. The
movement spread rapidly throughout the world. Various
projects were initiated, concerned primarily with youth,

the family, the parish, different professions. The aim was to suggest new patterns of Christian life applicable at these various levels. It is too soon to write its full history, which is still being created under the action of the Spirit. But here, I think, we have a sign of hope for the Church. It was particularly visible last summer when some ten thousand young people from all over Europe gathered at Loppiano, the international training center near Florence.

It is difficult to appreciate, from reading alone, the freshness, the youth and the spirit of love that characterizes this movement: one must capture this on the spot, in day to day life. The basic idea is that the Church is a community of love in action. Going on from here, I would say that what strikes me most is a faith in the power of love as a revolutionizing force in the world; faith in the Gospel as a word of life, faith in the presence of Jesus where two or three are gathered in his name; faith in the power of the redemptive death of Jesus in his total abandonment on the cross and faith in the spiritual motherhood of Mary.

Remarkable also, in recent years, has been this movement's ecumenical dimension. It counts among its members non-catholic Christians, and organizes in its Roman headquarters at Rocca di Papa, regular meetings with Anglicans and Lutherans. One day, no doubt, someone will write the moving story of the relationshp between the Patriarch Athenagoras and Chiara Lubich, one which was a symbol of that visible unity which we are still seeking. This same ecumenical orientation is the inspiration of a new community venture in Ottmaring, not far from Augsburg in Germany, where Focolarini and Lutherans share a community life in a spirit of rare fraternal love.

The spirituality of the movement is having an ever increasing influence, spreading by a kind of osmosis throughout the Church: it seems it touches many different religious congregations and is finding a home in the most varied cultural environments. It bears witness to the Absolute, to God, "in deed and in truth."

The family provides the primary experience of Christian community. The Council said of it: "The family is, so to speak, the domestic Church." [15] It is also the starting point for all other community life. During the course of an address given to the Committee for the Family, Pope Paul spoke of the meaning of family in these words: "The home is the privileged place of love, of intimate communion between persons of apprenticeship in the continual, progressive self-giving of husband and wife to each other, and it must be firmly based on the unity and indissolubility of their marriage-bond. This love necessarily presupposes tenderness, self-control, patient understanding, faithfulness and generosity constantly renewed at the supernatural sources of their sacrament." [16]

Whatever strengthens the union between husband and wife, is a force which builds society.

A Jesuit priest, Gabriel Calvo, was responsible within the family movement in Spain for a remarkable enterprise, the precise purpose of which is to give fresh life to love in marriage and to renew through a deeper understanding of its meaning the bond between husband and wife. This valuable sharing of experience, known as "Marriage Encounter" is spreading at the present time to an astonishing degree, especially in the U.S.A. where it started among Spanish-speaking citizens. It was soon a dynamic force within the American Church at large, where some one hundred twenty thousand couples are already involved.

What is a "marriage encounter"? It begins with a simple fact: there is often a lack of real communication between married couples, even in good solid marriages. Experience shows that, over a period of years, married life can become a routine coexistence in which each spouse is preoccupied with a series of duties, which leave no time for a deep sharing of personal life in all its dimensions. If married love is to be genuine, it must be a communion of soul, spirit, heart and body.

Communion of soul means that life is really shared in its depth, and that both partners are able to mutually communicate what is deepest within them.

Communion of spirit means deep oneness in the way they both look at life and its fundamental problems. St. Exupéry wrote: "To love is not to gaze at each other, but to look outward, together, in the same direction." [17]

Communion of heart means mutual affection, gift of self, sharing in full the existence of the other.

Communion of body means physical union as the bodily expression of the sentiments of the soul.

The tragedy of our world today is that it disrupts and disintegrates the essential harmony of these elements and puts such a stress on the physical dimension that love becomes a caricature and nothing more than a juxtaposition of egoisms. In a word, love must be saved from all that threatens it, and love must be rediscovered deep in the heart of man.

This is the objective to which "Marriage Encounter" tries to respond and its success is impressive. Its method is a weekend retreat under the direction of two or three married couples and a priest. This is followed up by periodic meetings together. The teaching given embraces all that is sound in human experience and psychology and pursues this right to the very heart of all true communion, to God himself.

One realizes here to what extent the Holy Spirit, who is the "We," the living bond between the Father and the Son, is also the bond between husband and wife. It is he who brings to life the sacramental grace of marriage, bestowing on it a charismatic quality. Testimonies abound of married couples who have found again at a new depth, their unity in the Spirit, and who have come away from these weekends with a wholly new outlook, a wholly new joy: sure signs of the Spirit. I have heard many of these testimonies myself since the movement has been introduced in my diocese. I had followed a retreat of this type in the United States, "incognito" with one of my priests, so as to study at first hand "marriage encounter" and see what it could bring to married couples, but also how the "encounter" method could be applied to other human relationships. I feel convinced it could be adapted for persons living in community. When we returned to Belgium, I released from his other duties the priest who had been with me. He now devotes his full time to this apostolate, helped by a team of priests and teams of married couples. Over two thousand couples in Belgium have already had the experience of this renewal. I can only affirm that the finger of God is there, that a breath of spring is blowing over the wide field of family life, which badly needs to be renewed and lived in a truly Christian climate.

This movement too, has its ecumenical dimension. It is a privileged meeting place for Christians of different traditions. Without doctrinal compromise or an impoverishing "common denominator," each one feels at ease. Rediscovering human unity at its very source in God can only help Christians to feel more deeply the roots of their own Christian unity, their oneness in the Spirit.

The Holy Spirit and the Christian in the World

*The greatest gift Christians
can make to their fellow men
is to give a meaning
to the world, and to give this
meaning in Jesus.*
MARCEL LÉGAUT

I. A CONFLICT SITUATION.

A believer must live his Christian authenticity before the
Lord in the midst of a community of brothers and sisters,
but also in the midst of the world and in solidarity with all
mankind. This creates a state of tension. Jesus asked his
disciples to be the salt of the earth; he never promised they
would be in the majority; on the contrary, the very image
of salt does not suggest immensity. Jesus also used the
image of leaven in dough. The very nature of leaven
presents a contradiction, in that the leaven is, at one and
the same time, within the dough, of a different nature from
it, and even outside it, though in partnership with it; for
only then will the dough rise. Within. Different. Outside.

This is implicated in the invitation the Lord addresses to
his own. He asks them, at the same time to be in the world,
with the world, yet not of the world, so as to help our
brothers transcend their human limitations. Incarnation,
conflict, transcendence, these are facets of one same duty.

A Christian, who wants to assume the world, must
consider what Jesus himself did. Namely, by the incarnation, he came on earth, "for us men and for our salvation."
No one was ever more human than Jesus: he is a brother
to all men. The Holy Spirit covered Mary with his
shadow; a sign and a promise of presence and solidarity
with us. Apart from sin, "nothing truly human was foreign
to him". He came to accomplish a work of redemption,
salvation, a liberation from our sins, our miseries and
death. His life conflicts with the forces of evil and the sins
of the world. His struggle against the world reached its
climax on Good Friday on Golgotha. Now, the disciple is
not above his Master; he must follow in the footsteps of
Jesus and live in keeping with his call to be present to the
world, in all the clarity of the Gospel—the whole Gospel.
Jesus promised to send us his Spirit for that purpose, till
the end of time.

TENSIONS.

It is not surprising that these manifold demands cause
tensions; depending on whether, a Christian, by priority,
considers himself a man among other men or specially
anointed as a Christian, for a specific role.

We touch a delicate point on asking the question: a
Christian—let us say workman, journalist, industrialist—is
he a Christian workman, a Christian journalist, a Christian
industrialist, or a worker, a journalist, an industrialist who
happens to be a Christian? Our choice of the term
"Christian," whether as an adjective or noun, reveals how

we look upon the Christian in the world: what is at stake? Should the accent be put, first, on the fact that a man is a Christian, or that he belongs to this or that profession?

Hence the question: "Of these two propositions, which are not exclusive, which is the primary viewpoint, the direction in which we should look?" In the Gospel, Jesus underlines that there exists between him and his disciples a deep spiritual solidarity that goes beyond the natural ties of flesh and blood, and that this can demand many sacrifices. Think afresh of the scene in the Gospel where someone comes to tell Jesus that his mother and brothers would like to speak to him. He replies: "My mother and my brothers are those who hear the word of God and put it into practice" (Lk. 8, 19–21).

Another aspect of this tension is there again when a Christian, thinking of the Church, sees it first and foremost as an inner reality, a mystery of God or as a service to mankind, springing up from man's initiative. It is essential to balance these two aspects of the Church in a well thought out synthesis.

Vatican II has assessed the Church in itself as the mystery of its own being, in the Constitution *Lumen Gentium. Gaudium et Spes* considered the Church as a reality in this world. These two documents do not correspond with one another perfectly—just as if a telescope had not been perfectly focused. The very nature of the Council's way of working did not permit a perfectly balanced synthesis: after all, a Council is not a Faculty of Theology in a University. Then, too, *Gaudium et Spes* was, for the first time in history, an attempt to deal explicitly with relations between the Church and the world. I think that even if it lacks the theological density of *Lumen Gentium, Gaudium et Spes* has blazed a trail that we must follow. In particular, we must attempt to elaborate a synthesis between what is immanent and what is transcendent in the Church's presence in the world. The problems of their interpenetration are at the heart of our divisions and of many of our conflicts.

In a text, quoted earlier, Paul Ricoeur showed the danger of divergences between Christians on the very meaning of Christianity. He continues:

"Another fissure is observable between the two functions of the institution itself: care for internal cohesion, and care for service to the world. The first preoccupation, were it to remain exclusive, results in what I would roughly call internal consumption. The second, separated from the first, tends to merge the Church into the world, which is one way to make salt lose its savour. Is it not an urgent task of the Church today to maintain balance between these two tensions? After all, why preserve the Church's specificity if not to serve others? And, on the other hand, what service will the Church be if it has nothing unique to offer?" [1]

IMAGES OF THE CHURCH.

At the Council, I suggested that we distinguish between the Church within itself, "*ad intra*," and the Church in relation to the outside world, "*ad extra*." The distinction had the advantage of clarifying some issues and of providing a practical basis for a division of work. It is, however, only a schema, since these two facets necessarily overlap.

We can, of course, put the emphasis on one or on the other. Some people think of the Church as primarily for the world and for the role it has to play in the world, and they begin from here when attempting to define it. Others see it primarily in relation to Jesus and the Spirit, which gives it life, and they tend to define the Church intrinsically as the leaven before they think of the leaven in the dough. This, again, is in the nature of a schema and it will, undoubtedly be the work of the theologians of tomorrow to harmonize and at least make more explicit these two complementary facets of the Church. For what service can the Church render to the world if it ceases to be itself and gets lost in the world under the pretext of helping it? The image then of the Church, that is put in relief, inevitably conditions subsequent discussions and controversies.

On the one hand, a "closed circuit" Church runs the risk of fostering a disembodied piety, making the Christian a stranger among his fellowmen.

On the other hand, a Church open to the four winds, immersed in the world, runs the risk in its effort to be totally human of becoming a complement and an extension of the existing social and political activities of persons who can more and more easily do without a Church.

This is the permanent dilemma of the Church. It is in the world and for the world, but not of the world, and there are areas of life where it has to be against the world, so as to be faithful to the Gospel. The paradoxical image of the leaven always holds good: it must be right inside the dough—not a fraction of an inch away—if it is going to be of any use. It must on the other hand remain leaven and keep all its own energy if it is not to be smothered and reduced to nothing by the resistance of the dough.

This is not a new problem. It is the endless conflict between the "natural" and the "supernatural" viewpoint. The first stresses so much the need to insert the Church in the world that there is a risk of the Church's losing its identity and compromising the transcendence of the Gospel. The second priding itself on being intransigent, sets the sphere of grace so far beyond the reach of ordinary life, that it fails to make itself heard by the world and thus proves false to the basic logic of the Gospel incarnating the Christ-life. No one, of course, confesses to be a pure "naturalist" or "supernaturalist." Each one tries to steer a course between Scylla and Charybdis with greater or with less success. A Christianity that has become too humanistic and too political is in perpetual conflict with a Christianity that is cut off from its temporal roots in the world, centered too much in the sanctuary of the temple, and not enough in the market place.

II. AN AMBIGUITY TO BE REMOVED.

Today the Church is often criticized for being so preoccupied with problems of an internal and purely ecclesiastical nature that it fails to be open to the world, and sufficiently involved with mankind. This impression of a "self-centered Church" is heightened by the mass-media which loudly announce the slightest changes in the ritual or the calendar and give to these secondary, peripheral matters a disproportionate importance.

On the other hand, if complete indifference is shown in regard to the Church *at intra*, it often springs from an unconscious notion that what transpires within the Church has no outside repercussions. However, this is to forget that very often things which touch the interior life of the Church have a determining effect on its exterior mission. Certain decisions regarding procedure within make the Church more open, more relevant, to people in the world. In this sense, the Church resembles the St. Gothard tunnel which links Switzerland and Italy. Any work done inside this tunnel to strengthen the arches, repair the rails or to clear away obstacles, automatically means easier access for everyone, no matter from which end of the tunnel they begin.

This was clearly seen at the time of the Council. If the world press gave a good deal of publicity—and it was generally favourably disposed—to the affairs of the Council, it was because it sensed, though in a confused sort of way, that the problems of the Church touch the lives of men and women, and that the Christian message has something to say to the world. Moreover, no one can forget the impact made by Pope John XXIII's encyclical *Pacem in Terris*, which recalled in a simple and direct style, the eternal message of the Gospel.

III. THE LORD, SENT INTO THE WORLD UNDER THE MOVEMENT OF THE HOLY SPIRIT.

To understand better the mission of a Christian in the world, let us turn our thoughts to our Lord Jesus Christ, just as he was beginning his public mission.

St. Luke first describes the baptism of Jesus in the Jordan, where the Holy Spirit "descended on him in bodily shape, like a dove." Then, he tells us "Jesus, full of the Holy Spirit, left the Jordan and was led by the Spirit into the wilderness . . ." (Lk. 4, 1). After this, Jesus, in the power of the Spirit, returned to Galilee. Having come to Nazareth, he went into the synagogue on the sabbath day and stood up to read. He was handed the scroll of the prophet Isaiah. He opened the scroll and found the passage which says:

> "The Spirit of the Lord has been given to me,
> for he has anointed me.
> He has sent me to bring the good news to the poor,
> to proclaim liberty to captives
> and to the blind new sight,
> to set the downtrodden free,
> to proclaim the Lord's year of favour" (Lk. 4, 16–21).

This passage described so vividly his mission, that when he had finished reading, he said to those listening: "This text is being fulfilled today even as you hear" (Lk. 4, 21).

What strikes one most in St. Luke's verses is his insistence that Jesus went out to people, moved by the Holy Spirit. We know, of course, that the Holy Spirit had overshadowed Mary with his power, and that from the moment of his conception, Jesus was already anointed by the Spirit: we are here at the heart of our faith.

It is helpful to reflect that we are not called "Jesusites" but "Christians," taking our name not from "Jesus," but from "Christ," that is "the Anointed One," whom "God anointed with the Holy Spirit" (Acts 10, 38). The humanity of Jesus was, one might say, penetrated by the Holy Spirit; he was guided by the Spirit at every stage of his life, up to his supreme act of love: the giving up of himself to death. And this is the same Spirit whom he promised to his own, to continue his work:

" 'If any man is thirsty, let him come to me!
Let the man come and drink who believes in me'
As Scripture says: 'From his breast shall flow fountains of living water.'
He was speaking of the Spirit which those who believed in him were to receive; for there was no Spirit as yet, because Jesus had not yet been glorified" (Jn. 7, 37–39).

These words of Jesus shed light on the Acts of the Apostles, and on every Christian life. As we discover afresh the role of the Holy Spirit, we will draw close to all persons. A paradox? We are inclined to forget the words of Isaiah read by Jesus in the synagogue, which began: "The Spirit of the Lord is given to me, for he has anointed me." Everything that Jesus did for his people, he did under the movement of the Holy Spirit, by the wisdom and the power of God. This intimate and profound union with the Spirit, this total concentration on obedience to the Father, far from taking Jesus away from our sufferings, plunged him into their reality. Each stage of his life in the mystery of the Incarnation, from the dawn of the Annunciation to the consummation on the cross, is penetrated by the power of the Holy Spirit.

IV. THE CHRISTIAN IN THE WORLD LED BY THE SPIRIT.

We too, baptized "in water and the Holy Spirit" have to live in the world as did Jesus: in communion with the world, at variance with it, transcending it. The Christian is at one and the same time, with, against, and beyond the world. The Holy Spirit is the living and integrating source of these three relations.

PRESENT TO THE WORLD.

The Spirit does not only speak in the silence of prayer. He speaks through the whole of human history; and to each generation he speaks a new language. To our generation, he speaks through the prodigious human enrichment in human knowledge; through the anguished searching and groping of man confronted with problems which surpass all that we were ever confronted with before; we tremble when we think of possible consequences of the power released by nuclear energy and atomic bombs.

The Holy Spirit, known or unknown, is at work within every effort being made to bring more light, sincerity, understanding, and peace among men. St. Ambrose used to say that whatever is true, by no matter whom it is said, is from the Holy Spirit; and St. Paul reminds us: "And now, my friends, all that is true, all that is noble, all that is just and pure, all that is lovable and gracious, whatever is excellent and admirable: fill all your thoughts with these things. The lessons I taught you, the tradition I have passed on, all that you heard me say or saw me do, put into practice, and the God of peace will be with you" (Phil. 4, 8–9).

This is the luminous side of the world. The creating

Spirit is present in the heart of his creation. For he is not only the soul of the Church, he is the soul of the world, animates every effort to renew the face of the earth. Perhaps, as someone said, we are still at the first day of creation.

SIGNS OF THE TIMES.

The Spirit invites us—the Council reminded us of this—to read "the signs of the times" and interpret them in the light of the Gospel. We know the answer given by Karl Barth, when asked how he prepared his sermons: "I take the Bible in one hand, the newspaper in the other, then read the paper in the light of the Word of God." This is how to interpret events day by day: God is there, under the guise of a duty, an emergency, a call for help.

The Holy Spirit is with us, revealing himself to us in our daily lives. He asks us to assume our Christian responsibilities, in every dimension, not only personal and family, but social, professional and political, on a local and a world-wide scale. In our day, as J. M. Domenach has well observed, "The great options of collective charity must be expressed in terms of political decisions." It may be difficult and laborious to arrive at such choices: situations are complex, and very often there will be conflicting duties. But whatever the concrete choice—and not to choose is already a choice—we need a Christian faith that is open to God in himself and listening to God in our fellow men and women. We have to learn how to integrate prayer and political action, prayer and social responsibility, prayer and justice, prayer and peace, prayer and the reconciliation of men.

We have to learn how to place our hope in what lies beyond, and at the same time work at what is in front of us, and thus build the Kingdom of God. True Christian hope does not supplant our hopes for here and now; on the contrary, it should be their incentive. As Roger Garaudy has put it:

"It is certain that Christian hope becomes alienation each time a Christian thinks that turning toward God means turning his back on the world. As if one could reach the "Kingdom of God" without passing through the transformation of the world. Such an attitude is being relegated more and more to the past. Many are the Christians today who are aware that the "other world" does not exclude, but even requires, a "different world." These Christians do not share a dualistic outlook which opposes the other world and this one; they do not think that God has created a ready-made universe."

Garaudy then goes on to condemn marxist hope as equally alienating, "each time it gives in to the illusion of thinking that by changing the system of private ownership, or even some more widespread system of social relationships, a 'new man' will necessarily come forth."[2]

A LETTER ABOUT THE SOCIAL DIMENSION
OF CHRISTIANITY.

One of our most dedicated young priests, who spent himself in the apostolate of social action in my diocese, wrote me a letter just before his death. These words of André Charlier will remain for us, his friends, as a final testament. I would like to share them here:

"I believe that one should insist, again and again, on the social dimension of Christianity. It is true that we hear a great deal about each one's personal relationship with God and about our horizontal relationships with one another. But it seems to me that it is all too rare that anyone speaks about the social dimension, the political aspect of love and Christian commitment. I think it is serious when we see so few Christians involved in political life, the drug problem, eroticism in our society, the lack of a professional future for our young people, the problem of the rights and duties of strikers, the need of new jobs etc. Too many Christians seem to think that these things have nothing to do with the Kingdom of God: and the too rare Christians who try are soon condemned as marxists.

On the contrary, I think Christians have to be reminded that they have a constant duty, especially in community action to continually assess their commitment and have the courage to take a look at it in the light of the Gospel, especially the beatitudes.

"In brief, I would say that there are two mistakes in store for modern Christians: either a Christianity with no body . . . or a Christianity with no Christ."

Then, further on in his letter he proclaims his faith in the resurrection and in the Holy Spirit:

"We have to reveal the silent presence of the risen Christ who is truly *alive*, and is a moving force at the heart of a humanity which is suffering, struggling, hoping."

A SPECIFIC KIND OF PRESENCE.

A real Christian presence in the world cannot be shamefaced or sold cheap. We have to bring to our fellow humans our greatest treasures: that is, a power and wisdom greater than our own, which brings liberation and salvation. Recall the scene at the 'Gate of the temple which is called Beautiful,' when a crippled beggar looked at Peter and John, hoping for alms. Peter said to him: "I have neither silver nor gold, but I will give you what I have: in the name of Jesus Christ the Nazarene, walk!" (Acts 3, 6) This should be for us, who believe in the Resurrection, the ultimate Christian response.

For the believer, Jesus himself is the decisive answer to the problems of the world. He is, in person, the wisdom and the power of God. We put our confidence in *him*, and not only in the principles and values found in his Gospel: we must ask him to teach us himself how to apply the power and the wisdom of God to our problems here-and-now.

The Christian has a specific service to render to the world. This should not hinder his collaboration with others not connected with the Church. Here confusion is very common: Christians are tempted to put their faith in parentheses, or to soft-pedal it in order to work better alongside others in the accomplishment of some goal. They forget that they have to be loyal at one and the same time, to their baptism and their solidarity with all mankind; not rarely they tend to sacrifice Christian fidelity here and adopt purely human means to carry out some project. In every age, the Church is invited to renounce her own identity under pretext of thus being more effective. It is the temptation to look for rich and powerful means of winning the world for Christ; forgetting that the Gospel proclaims the incomparable power of poverty. Every answer that Jesus gave to the tempter in the desert warns us to be on our guard against this. As Bishop Matagrin of Grenoble wrote:

"Let us be on our guard against confusing the renewal of the Church with the transformation of society. More and more people are beginning to question a society that is founded on money, prestige and power, and are striving to build a society that has more respect for man, is founded on liberty, justice and solidarity. The members of the Church are invited to help with this task in the name of what love and hope require of them. However, if this effort to transform mentalities, life styles and structures really expresses the fruits of the Holy Spirit, then it has its source and meaning only within the Spirit himself. The word "liberation" can frequently be a trap, since it can be applied to political transformation or to evangelical conversion." [3]

A social vocation is not at all the same as a religious vocation—we have to keep the distinction here. All

confusion on these levels weakens the significance and
stifles the awakening of religious vocations, which far
surpass a call to social action. As Marcel Légaut has put
it: "There is a great temptation in groups of the sociologi-
cally minded to substitute a current ideology for the
Gospel, and to make of this ideology the centre of their
lives, even though they still use Christian terminology".[4]
The Christian should plunge into the sea of the world, yet
he must avoid baptism by immersion!

QUESTIONING THE WORLD.

There is a mysterious text in the Gospel of St. John,
where he says of the Holy Spirit: "And when he comes, he
will convince the world of sin and of righteousness and of
judgment" (Jn. 16, 8). This is not an easy text to interpret,
though its general sense is clear: the Holy Spirit manifests
Christ, and, by contrast, shows all that is opposed to him.
He thus reveals the iniquity of the world, and his
condemnation of it and shows up evil in its true light.
What is more, such a revelation makes clear the defeat of
the prince of this world, who, by instigating Jesus' death,
worked his own ruin.

The Spirit does not only explore the depths of God, he
also explores the depths of a man's heart. The light of the
Spirit is our guide as we make our way through the world,
which is in rebellion against God and is plunged in
darkness—that world for which Jesus did not pray (Jn. 17,
9). This world, Alas! exists today, and it would be a
serious lack of realism to try to ignore it. Sociology should
do its task and analyze the sources of our social inequali-
ties, and propose necessary structural reforms: that is its
function. But we can never forget that all reforms, all
regimes we may introduce, will always be fragile because
threatened by the evil that is in man himself.

THE SOURCE OF EVIL.

Racial or group hatred, personal or collective egoism, violence which breeds violence, moral profligacy and commercial fraud, hypocrisy and lies: all these vitiate the functioning of institutions and compromise efforts to improve them. Evils like these are not healed by passing a new law. The ultimate problem from which we suffer lies neither in our institutions nor in things: it is within us, in our hearts and in our souls. This interior evil is the reason why the same social abuses arise over and over again, no matter what social system is tried. Because we do not try to change the source of injustice itself, all our efforts only serve to make it change position.

We can never stress enough how sin itself is anti-social. It craftily embroils human relationships and compromises the humanization of the world. Faith tells us, more, that it embroils the whole mystical Body of Christ—that every sin, in a mysterious way, reinforces the hold Satan has over the world. The real crisis in the world is a spiritual one, and the theatre in which this drama is performed none other than the human conscience. Still, the effects of this interior drama end always by manifesting themselves in the world of events. Sin, nihilistic by its very nature, shakes the world to its very foundations, whereas the grace of God renews the world and brings it to a higher state of perfection, individual and collective.

Thanks to our faith, we know that no name other than that of Jesus, can, in the last analysis, bring salvation. Without him, we only touch the surface. There is a Christian way of working for the promotion of what is human, whether we are concerned with education, health, or the development of the third world. This does not in any way exclude close cooperation of Christians with all men of good-will, especially in a pluralistic society such as our own. Christians must not shut themselves up in ghettos. They must remember that always and everywhere, they are, in consequence of their baptism, under the guidance of the Holy Spirit. No matter what the problem with which they are faced, they must believe, in faith, that the power and wisdom of the Spirit of God are there to guide and strengthen them. It is not for nothing that the liturgy teaches us to pray: "Come Holy Spirit, and renew the face of the earth." This presence of the Spirit in us is like a beam from a lighthouse, which, in the darkness of the night, sheds its light upon the shore and reveals dangers and hidden reefs concealed from us. It helps us to see more clearly whatever is inhuman in our society. It forces us to face the fact that conformity with society, hides the depths of our cowardice, our concern for human respect, our fear: it reveals to us the false gods of our day and denounces our successive forms of idolatry. The gods of today are no longer called Baal and Astarte; their names are a society dominated by profit, a permissive society at the mercy of every passing whim. We give them our tacit approval every time we yield, for fear of "something worse."

At one time, Christians were put to death for refusing to offer a few grains of incense to an idol. Today's Caesars do not have a name of their own: they are called power, money, pleasure. Rosemary Haughton has spoken, quite rightly, about the "opting out" of too many Christians in society today:

"So perhaps we shall have to stop being good citizens, if the city belongs to the Prince of this world. We may have to stop being respectable and approved. It hasn't happened for a long time. It could be happening now, and we need to be aware of this change; because if we aren't, then we may wake up one day and find we aren't Christians any more, but only good, respectable citizens." [5]

GOING BEYOND THE WORLD.

This world will pass away: we know that we are on a journey toward the end of time, toward a meeting with the Lord who will wipe away every tear from our eyes, there where death will be no more, and God will be all in all. We are a pilgrim Church, making our way toward the full revelation of God, toward the hour when, "there shall be no more night, nor will they need the light of lamp or sun, for the Lord God will give them light" (Rev. 22, 5).

We must keep in our heart a living hope that carries us on towards the ultimate manifestation of God's glory and at the same time gives us the insight and the courage to work at making this world a better place to live in. Our vision of the future ought to increase the value of the present, in our eyes, not lessen it. Every effort to make this life more human is worthwhile, and is already a foretaste of the "new heaven and new earth" that awaits us. We must, at the same time, move toward a future that surpasses all our dreams, and at the same time be sincerely involved in God's "today" at the heart of the world.

We should not, however, read into every disaster, signs that prophesy the end of the world.

There is a fundamentalist style of writing which cheapens the predictions in the Scriptures and is not really faithful to their message. The Church wisely urges prudence in these matters, in keeping with the words of Jesus who, asked about the end of time, said it was the secret of his Father. We must guard against irresponsible apocalyptic forecasts: God's thoughts are beyond our understanding, but his will for us for today is clear. He wills that we go forward along the road that leads to a meeting with him: "until he comes," and that we travel in the joy of the Spirit, who whispers within us: "Come, Lord Jesus" (Rev.

22, 17.20). But he also wills that we be fully aware of the sufferings of our fellowmen, and that we work along with them to build a new world. True piety will never be an escape.

The Holy Spirit
and Ecumenical Hopes

*The whole (ecumenical) enterprise is the
Holy Spirit who is the Spirit of truth and the
Spirit of love, working in us, uniting us in
love and building us up in the truth. Those
are the things that matter. We must avoid
binding the Spirit by our stupidity and
narrowness and lack of faith.*
ARCHBISHOP MICHAEL RAMSEY[1]

The second Vatican Council recognized in the stirrings of
ecumenism throughout the world a sign of the active
presence of the Holy Spirit in the Church. There were
some important texts adopted during the Council which
expressed a sense of openness and receptivity in our
relationships with other Christian Churches. A Secretariat
of Christian Unity was established which, under the
present leadership of Cardinal Willebrands, takes many
initiatives and multiplies contacts with our non-Catholic
brethren. Then too, in different countries, groups of
theologians have worked out together doctrinal state-

ments. Significant steps therefore have been taken toward a mutual understanding.

In Belgium, in 1971, a statement worked out in common, concerning baptism conferred by the various Christian Churches, was an important landmark in our ecumenical history.[2] In England, in 1971, the Windsor Statement on Eucharistic Doctrine was agreed upon between Anglicans and Roman Catholics. In France, the Dombes Statement (September 1971) moves in the same direction. Recently a significant text has been published, summarizing the findings of a commission held by Lutherans and Roman Catholics on the theme: "The Gospel and the Church."[3] Here again, the large zones of agreement were impressive. There was understanding on both sides as to the ministry and useful suggestions offered to bring nearer the time when intercommunion will be possible. This is the place to mention, too, in relation to the question of ministry, *The Canterbury Statement on Ministry and Ordination*, published by the Anglican-Roman Catholic International Commission.

What is the significance of this statement? Herbert Ryan, S.J., who was closely associated with the drafting of the document, replies:

"What are the 'agreed statements' meant to be? They are not to be doctrinal treaties or decrees drawn up by ARCIC and submitted to Church authorities with the intention that they promulgate them as binding on Church members. Though the agreed statements ought to reflect the best contemporary scholarship on the issues studied, they are not meant to be scholarly discourses which would interest onl professional academics trained in theology and history. The agreed statements are study documents . . . (They) are models of ecumenical, theological dialogue to which Anglicans and Roman Catholics are invited to respond prayerfully, thoughtfully, and critically. The purpose of the agreed statements is both to foster and to express doctrinal consensus between the Roman Catholic Church and the Anglican Communion."[4]

We could go on giving examples of these converging lines, but perhaps these are sufficient. The dialogue has not ended. We must now move on to the next stage, to the problems of ecclesiology, such as the primacy of Peter and collegiality in the Church. But already the ground has been cleared. Pope Paul VI traced the route to be followed when not long ago he said in an allocution:

"There is no dialogue possible without a deepened understanding of our interlocutor, or as it is said today, of 'the other.' This noble enterprise demands an optimistic view of man; it is a true asceticism! We must surmount the barriers imposed by language and cultural patterns of thought, going beyond polemics and mistrust, so that we be open to true universality." [5]

Some time ago, the anglican bishop Dr. Mervyn Stockwood, sent me an article of his that appeared in *The Catholic Herald*.[6] He suggests under seven headings ecumenical proposals to be adopted, by Anglicans and Roman Catholics alike: they are an urgent moving invitation to advance further in the direction in which we have begun. I cannot here take up each proposal, but I would like to say that I gladly subscribe to the first which is, in a way, the key to all the others: "We should not do separately what, in good conscience, we can do together." And this takes us a long way.

FEARS.

Despite undeniable activity and mutual good-will, the ecumenical movement seems nevertheless to show signs of stagnation. This impression can be explained to some degree by the fact that its sensational aspects have died down. Ecumenism can be compared to "taking off" in a "jet" plane. As we leave the ground, the engines make a tremendous roar. Then, once the plane is airborne, there is silence; it is hard to realize that we are moving at all. Now and again, an "air pocket" and the pilot telling us to fasten our seat-belts, is a reminder that we are in flight.

The ecumenical movement gathered momentum in the Catholic Church during the years 1960–1970. And it had its spectacular moments. There were the meetings, one after another between Pope Paul VI and the Patriarch Athenagoras in Jerusalem, Constantinople, Rome. And world-wide coverage in the press. Then silence. The publication of the *Book of Charity*, in 1972, brought to light some three hundred documents exchanged between Rome and Constantinople during the last few years. But this passed without a sound; we were at an altitude beyond the reach of the mass media. Once in a while, we encounter "air pockets" in the ecumenical atmosphere, but these pass. One of the most dangerous threats to ecumenism was, I would say, the proposal two years ago, to introduce a *Lex Ecclesiae Fundamentalis*: a sort of Constitution for the Church. For the moment that danger, it seems, has passed. But it would be wise to keep our seat-belts fastened!

There was fresh consternation in ecumenical circles— one cannot pretend otherwise—at the publication of the document *Mysterium Ecclesiae*, June 24, 1973. Its phrasing concerning the unique Church of the Lord seemed, in some ways, a step back as compared to the conciliar statement which was much more nuanced on this point. Further, this new document was not in harmony with other documents and attitudes of the Holy See. However, in other respects what is said in this same document, about historical contingency and the formulation, not the content, of dogmatic statements could be a help in ecumenical dialogue. The future will dispel the unease which, we know from their reactions, was felt in some non-Roman quarters. Whatever may be the exact exegesis of the text, I do not think it should be interpreted as a set-back to ecumenical efforts.[7]

No, ecumenism has not run out of fuel; the plane is still in midflight. From time to time, through an opening in the clouds we glimpse flat countries where we will be able tomorrow to lay out an air-strip.

The drive toward unity among Christians seems irreversible: we may hope that the hour is not far off. The first millennium was, with some exceptions, the era of the undivided Church. The second, from 1054 until now, has seen the Church torn asunder. We are permitted to be confident with hope founded in God and in the progress of theology that the third millennium will see the restoration of full unity and full communion.

Nevertheless, this hope of ours encounters obstacles of many kinds which it would be foolish to minimize. I will examine two of them. Beginning from opposite premises, both give cause to fear.

ALLERGIES TO ECUMENISM.

Among the younger generation of both lay people and clerics, especially among those involved in social questions, there is a disturbing lack of interest. It applies to clergy and laity alike. They are allergic to ecumenism which they see as being concerned with long out-dated quarrels: they think it would be better to let the dead bury their dead. The past is no concern of theirs. Their thoughts are on the future, and when we are rejoicing at efforts being made in common which have brought together Christians of all confessions, they remain scandalized by our unbelievable inertia and tenacious animosities.

Again, young people are not interested in doctrinal issues: theological discussions do not fit into their mental framework. In a pragmatic world such as ours, affairs of a doctrinal order are *ipso facto* viewed with disfavour.

Another point. Ecumenical problems are also institutional: the ultimate purpose of our discussions can only be the definition of the organic unity we are attempting to achieve. We know how allergic many of our contemporaries are to anything that has to do with institutions. The liberty of the Spirit, as our young people see it, sweeps away structures. This disaffection extends not only to Churches, but also to the World Council of Churches, which seems to them too ponderous to be moved by the inspirations of the Spirit.

In brief, ecumenism has the great fault of being just another affair in which Churches are involved, whereas the Church of their dreams looks outwards, concerning itself entirely with the problems of the world. Our preoccupation with ecumenism appears to them as introversion. "Let us," they say, "go out altogether, to meet the needs of the world. This is what interests us. This, in our eyes, is what comes first." These are some of their reasons for keeping ecumenism at a distance.

The tension between the generations underlies this difference of opinion. This disdain for history, doctrine, institution and ecclesiology is regrettable to us for whom history remains a source of enlightenment; doctrine, a source of life; the institutional, an indispensable dimension of the Church, which must remain truly itself so as to be of service to the world.[8]

Ignorance of the factors that gave rise to our present situation is a block to the development of ecumenical dialogue. We ignore the past at our cost: it is the key to understanding the present. History is made up of a series of chain reactions. It is indispensable, if we are to understand the reason for schisms and rifts. History has liberated us, to our advantage, from the caricatures we have made of certain figures of the past: a Photius or a Luther. This obliges us to make new assessments. Moreover bringing to light the extent to which past controversies have been falsified, because the questions were posed in too narrow a context, opens new perspectives. And this is essential if we are to put in its right setting, a fragmentary truth that has been isolated, for want of a harmonious synthesis. History is a school in which we acquire a healthy relativity—I do not say relativism: it helps us separate the essential from what is contingent, transitory and conditioned by a sociological milieu. It allows us to get rid of our prejudice and predetermined attitudes. It teaches us humility—we all have to admit our faults—and the forbearance of God, in his dealings with us.

THE FEAR OF SECULARISM.

Looking in a quite different direction, we find those who fear that ecumenism should become purely secular, with all the attention of the Church concentrated on social commitment to the world. The Orthodox Churches, both Greek and Russian, are especially sensitive to this danger.[9] The twenty-fifth anniversary of the World Council of Churches (W.C.C.) was the occasion for issuing warnings in this regard. The encyclical Letter of the Orthodox Churches in America, in March 1973, the Patriarchs Pimen of Moscow and Dimitrios of Constantinople,[10] Archbishop Iakovos of the United States and Archbishop Athenagoras of Great Britain are alike in sounding the same warning against reducing the Christian faith to a kind of humanism and to human attitudes. Here, for example is a statement of Archbishop Iakovos:

"I am not suggesting in any way the World Council of Churches should show apathy or a lack of interest as to the evils which plague our society. Neither would I suggest that the Council ought to avoid taking a clear stand on and proclaiming loudly a Christian viewpoint regarding the flagrant violation of the most essential human rights."

But Archbishop Iakovos goes on to say:

"the Council should concentrate its attention on the theme of unity which is the main justification for the very existence of the Council. If ecumenism is a movement destined to mobilize and unite the Christian Churches in the same search, towards the same goal, that is, Christian unity, then all is well. But if ecumenism is envisaged as a movement whose first duty is to be opposed to capitalism, marxism, socialism, colonialism, and totalitarianism; if it must free society from all its "isms" in order finally to establish Christianity as an ideal way of life in the midst of human and international affairs, then the World Council of Churches would do well to examine again first of all its presuppositions, its capacities and its ambitions, however noble these may be." [11]

If one can criticize orthodoxy for not being sufficiently incarnate—and political situations are in part responsible for this—one should at least take orthodoxy's own expression of itself into account.[12]

We could give other reasons for ecumenical pessimism but these are enough to show that the road is not without its dangers. Ought we to speak of an impasse? I do not think so; and I would like to emphasize to what an extent our rediscovery of the presence of the Holy Spirit, experienced in our lives, is a great sign of hope. We can see a surprising convergence of the Christian Churches toward the Holy Spirit, who is, as it were, our meeting point, at the same time, on the levels of spirituality, doctrine and development.

I. A SPIRITUAL MEETING PLACE.

From the beginning of all ecumenical dialogue, we have to be aware that a dialogue of this kind is not something purely human: it is not merely a question of persons of good-will in search of an honorable diplomatic compromise. There is one over-riding consideration: the will of the Triune God.

At a retreat given to Roman Catholic clergy, an Episcopalian Bishop, Dr. Harvey Butterfield said: "It is terribly important for us to realize that what is happening in the Church is not to be confused with modernization. We are not trying to keep up with every avant-garde trend: we are trying to keep up with God! God is doing unprecedented things in our generations and we are being challenged to discern these things and respond to them."

We cannot say often enough: unity is a gift of God, a grace for which we should beg the Lord together. Moreover on the threshold of every ecumenical effort we should recall the words of Cardinal Bea: "The door to unity is entered on our knees."

We must pray together fervently. We do this during the Unity Octave from January 18 to 25 every year. This is a first step but still a timid and sporadic one. It is something, but we are not entering into God's own loving impatience. We too easily hide behind a patience we impose on him, forgetting that he "longs to eat the passover with us" (see Lk. 22, 15), the passover of unity.

Now, it is only the Spirit who can truly pray in us, and only he can bring us to the real depths of prayer and cause us to say the name of Jesus as Christians should, that is, together.

It is the Spirit who unites us in the acclamation "Jesus is Lord." He is amongst us at our meetings. For every real ecumenical dialogue is not primarily one between Churches. It is not a dialogue between Rome and Canterbury, Rome and Moscow, Rome and Geneva. It is rather an inner spiritual dialogue between Rome, Canterbury, Moscow, Geneva and our common Master: Jesus Christ. To the degree that the Spirit reveals to us the true face of Christ, no shadow will cloud our own: "Every face turned to him grows brighter, and is never ashamed" (Ps. 34, 5). By uniting ourselves to Christ, we have true communion with one another; this is the short way to unity. As Archbishop Ramsey has expressed it:

"The secret of coming nearer to one another is that we should all of us become nearer to Christ. He welcomes us to an amazing nearness to himself; that is the secret, if only we will receive his welcome.

"Yes, the reintegration of Christendom does not only mean the one dimension of our coming ecclesiastically closer to one another. If it meant only that it could never happen at all. No, the reintegration of Christendom includes the deeper union of all of us with Christ: Christ who is himself the heart of Catholic truth as Incarnate, Crucified, Risen, the Lord of his Church and the Lord of heaven; Christ who is himself the way of holiness." [13]

Prayer together, in which we open ourselves to the action of the Holy Spirit, is an ecumenical priority. This communal prayer to the Lord will confer on theological research which is indispensable, not just new energy but a new depth. And this prayer must not only introduce our work together, it should be part of the rhythm of our sessions, and would transform the whole atmosphere. Recently, I was present at some "planning" sessions during meetings of leaders in the Charismatic Renewal. These sessions not only opened with a long period of spontaneous prayer, but were interspersed with prayer on the invitations of the president, to ask the Lord to send his Spirit to enlighten us on the subject under discussion and the decisions to be made. Prayer and work were organically bound together in the meeting itself, and one sensed a moving atmosphere of trust and humility before the Lord. If only the Holy Spirit would preside in the same way at our ecumenical dialogues . . . and at others!

Would it not be wonderful, too, if there were more interchange of this kind between Church leaders, at diocesan and parochial levels, and that this were a means of bringing together Christians in a common prayer, nourished by the word of God? The Acts of the Apostles tell us that when Peter was in prison the whole Christian community "prayed to God for him unremittingly" (Acts 12, 5). Our prayer for the restoration of unity must be no less continuous, not only because this is our first step on the way of unity, but also because prayer is the indispensable climate that opens our hearts to its realization. We should not forget the painful experience of the Council of Florence concerning unity, in the fifteenth century. It failed to reconcile Catholics and Orthodox because, among other reasons, agreement was reached at the top, but the people had not been prepared for this nor were they associated with it.

This prayer shared with others can be encouraged by meeting in groups for spontaneous prayer, Charismatic or otherwise. These give an opportunity for frequent communion in spirit as we wait for the longed-for hour of Eucharistic intercommunion. Prayer in common, sustained by the word of God, is a never-failing spring where Christians of every confession can come and quench their thirst together in an atmosphere of respect and mutual love.

This does not mean that a badly understood charity should obliterate doctrinal divergencies not yet resolved. Everyone must preserve his own identity, while respecting that of others. On such occasions, for instance, Catholics should not minimize their beliefs or their devotion to Mary. The Spirit knows how to create harmonious prayer, if only every instrument is in tune.

II. A DOCTRINAL MEETING PLACE.

In an article entitled, "I believe in the Holy Spirit in the Church," [14] Yves Congar, O.P., wrote:

"Almost without exception, the Christians who are not in full communion with us, whether orthodox or protestant, reproach us for our deficient 'pneumatology.' They understand by this that we do not attribute to the Holy Spirit a real personal role, which is something more than simply carrying out, as an instrument, the work of Christ, or merely guaranteeing the correct functioning of the institution. This personal role of the Spirit seems to them to be implied in the liberty and personalization of grace.

"We might think that the reproach is exaggerated and therefore unjust. Nevertheless, we ought to admit that it has some foundation. We have spoken about the Holy Spirit in connection with the spiritual life, but except for his role in assuring the reality of the sacramental or hierarchical acts, we have not said much of the Spirit in our ecclesiology, at least until recently. The situation is improving with our deeper appreciation of the meaning of local communities, of the charisms, as well as with the renewal movement rich in initiatives."

It is indeed true that the situation is improving. The Council contributed to this by stressing the role of the Holy Spirit in some important texts. Since then, Pope Paul VI has said unequivocally that the work of Vatican II ought to be furthered by a more developed pneumatology, "as an indispensable complement of the teaching of the Council." We quoted this text in full in our first chapter.

These words of Pope Paul carry us far. Any development in pneumatology on the doctrinal level, is of its very nature, moving in the direction of ecumenical union. This does not mean that all of a sudden we will have no more theological clashes. It does mean, however, that we can meet on common ground—and this is important.

It is not difficult to look back over some of the controversies of the past and see how, if the role of the Holy Spirit had been given greater prominence, the atmosphere would have been less "charged," and different points of view brought closer to one another. For example, the restoration, in our new Eucharistic prayers, of a twofold explicit invocation of the Holy Spirit has, on the liturgical level, meant greater understanding between ourselves and our eastern brethren. Also, by emphasizing the presence of the Holy Spirit at the heart of the Church, our ecclesiology high-lights the charismatic dimension of the Church which is too often neglected and facilitates dialogue with our protestant brethren. And we could go on. . . .

In saying this, I do not deny or minimize the difficulties that remain unresolved on the institutional level, particularly whatever relates to the role of Peter's ministry in the Church. But, by giving priority to the role of the Holy Spirit, we have created a new perspective which serves to locate and limit some of our other problems. At the same time, it gives us a point of reference—a focal point—that enables us to talk more easily in a language familiar to all.

It is not my intention here to list the problems yet to be resolved, still less to propose solutions for each. I would like simply to share some reflections, which are not exhaustive, on the Holy Spirit as providing a doctrinal meeting place where certain crucial issues can be discussed.

In the first place, all of us together must put ourselves under the authority of the Word of God, expressed in a very special manner in the Scriptures which are inspired and illumined by the Holy Spirit. The dogmatic Constitution, on *Divine Revelation*, states that the teaching authority entrusted with the authentic interpretation of the Word of God, is not above the Word of God, but serves it, teaching only what has been handed on, listening to it devoutly, guarding it scrupulously and explaining it faithfully by divine commission and with the help of the Holy Spirit; it draws from this one deposit of faith everything which it presents for belief as divinely revealed.[15]

All of us are aware of the presence of the Holy Spirit at the very origins of Holy Scripture, even if the further theological explanations of this inspiration may be different. We believe together that the Spirit has spoken through the Scriptures, and we profess together that this same Spirit enlightens the souls of believers by a direct contact within us to which Scripture itself bears witness. We differ regarding the role and authority of the official teaching office in the interpretation of the Scriptures, and on the role of a living tradition which has been called the "epiclesis (invocation) of the Spirit." However, we are coming closer to one another in a deep-seated readiness, shared in common, to receive the Word of God.

Besides, rather than consider first of all a teaching Church over against a taught Church, we have become aware that we are all together a Church taught by the Holy Spirit. Within this fundamental perspective we see more clearly the distinction between the teaching Church and the Church that is taught. I say distinction, not separation. The bishops in collegial union with the Pope, their head, before becoming the teaching Church, were and remain, under some respects, the taught Church. They are the heirs of the theology of their time, and of their seminary, as well as the heirs of the spirituality of their era. All the bishops must first listen to the Holy Spirit so as to be able to speak according to their own particular charism, when there is question of the authenticity and interpretation of the Gospel message. The greater their mission, the greater their duty to listen. Fr. Bernard Haring once said: "Everyone recognizes—and rightly so—that the Pope, in a unique way, is the 'teaching Church.' But this is precisely what inspires him to be also in a unique way the 'taught Church.' He must be listening and ready to receive whatever in the Church is the fruit of the Spirit; he must take into account all the wealth of experience and the spiritual gifts of all the bishops and the people of God."

We all share the belief that Jesus has sent to us his Holy

Spirit to bring us more and more into the fullness of the truth which his disciples could not yet bear (see Jn. 16, 12). There is an interior dialogue, an anointing of the Spirit, which teaches each baptized person who is listening to God. There is a progressive revelation in fidelity, which the Spirit works each day in and through his Church. What the world expects of us in the first place is that we catch the sound of this voice of the Spirit, that we reveal the wisdom, the concern and the plan of God for humanity.

At the present time we are discovering more and more the meaning of communion in the Word of God. Not only in our worship, where the liturgy of the Word has recovered its range and true expression, but also in our community meetings where we share together the Word of God. We are discovering again that wealth of the Word as a means of entering into contact with God. The Lord can give to him who humbly asks and opens his Bible in faith, a word for the day, his daily bread, upon which he can reflect and be nourished. More and more we see Christians who carry with them a copy of the New Testament, and who find time each day to read it prayerfully. The Spirit speaks: experience shows that this is no illusion. Moreover to him who has already received even more will be given, freely and abundantly.

Let me illustrate this by a personal and ecumenical example. Some time ago, Dr. Michael Ramsey, the Archbishop of Canterbury visited me at Malines. Before beginning our conversation, I suggested we should pray together. We opened the Bible at the words: "Although the doors were locked, Jesus came and stood among them saying, 'Peace be with you' " (Jn. 20, 26). It seemed to us that this was an invitation of the Lord to continue our dialogue despite closed doors, knowing in our hearts that the Lord was being true to his word; that he was present because we had come together in his name.

III. ORGANIC UNITY AMONG THE CHURCHES.

The fundamental problem of ecumenism is that of restoring ecclesial unity. This implies that we have a clear vision of what unity really is, that we do not confuse it with uniformity, and that we know how to embrace a healthy pluralism. In the name of unity badly understood, there have been in the past many mistakes and fruitless tensions. We have only to recall the opposition to the Chinese rite that had been proposed by missionaries in the seventeenth century; the untoward manoeuvres to Latinize the oriental Church; the struggle at the Council against the monopoly of Latin in the liturgy; the struggle to allow the use of the vernacular; the difficult balance to maintain between collegiality and papal primacy. Little by little we are discovering, afresh, a vision which enables us to be open to legitimate diversity in a richer synthesis within the one Church of Christ.

Taking up the words of St. Cyprian of Carthage, Vatican II defined the Church as "a people made one with the unity of the Father, the Son, and the Holy Spirit." [16] It is natural that we should look to this primordial unity which commands our unity in the Church: the trinitarian unity. The ecclesial unity that we must try to restore as a visible reality should reflect the plural unity of God himself. At one time our theology so stressed the oneness of God that we ran the risk of looking upon him as uni-personal, and this had serious repercussions in our understanding of the Church as "the image of God."

In a recent interview, Father Heribert Muehlen developed this notion of the relation between God's inner life and our life in the Church. Answering a question concerning the new patterns of life he hoped to see emerge from the Charismatic Renewal, he replied:

"I think the Charismatic Renewal is God's response to what was called for in Vatican II as regards a more collegial, brotherly, communal way of making decisions and exercising authority in the church . . .

"When you see God as a community of persons, a community-oriented way of doing things is seen as more fitting. When church structure was being formed in the early second century, the great Trinitarian insights were not yet articulated. By the time they were, in the fourth century, it was too late to influence an already fixed style of doing things . . .

"The Holy Spirit is not simply a 'he,' but a 'we': the Father and Son coming to us, the dialogue of the Father and Son. I think of the Holy Spirit as the divine 'we,' so intensely does the Spirit make present to us the Father and Jesus, and so transparent is he in himself. He is the 'we' that makes us the people of God, one with the Father and Son. The Holy Spirit is also the ecclesial 'we.' When we say 'we' Christians, or 'we' the people of God, it is the Spirit within us that enables us to say 'we.' He is one person in many persons in the Church, one person in two other persons in the Trinity." [17]

We cannot minimize either the unity or the trinity in God, there is unity in trinity and trinity in unity.

Our ecumenical unity has its source in the mystery of the Trinity. Thus, it is easy to see how important it is to understand the role of the Spirit, the "we" of the Father and the Son, and the "we" of the Body of Christ. It is in this understanding that we can achieve that supernatural oneness that brings to perfection the individuality of each person and each tradition.

The Holy Spirit is, at the heart of the Church, creating a unity that transcends our calculations. We are seeing before our very eyes a converging action of the Spirit that permeates the different denominations. As Kevin Ranaghan writes:

"Jesus, our king, is determined to be Lord of all his people and he is pouring out his life-giving Spirit upon all our families. No matter what church background we may come from, no matter what feelings we may have had about each other, no matter what serious theological difficulties may still lie between us, Jesus is teaching us that we are basically and fundamentally called to be one people, one holy nation, one royal priesthood, a new humanity led by the New Adam. Regardless of our different denominations, we all know and accept Jesus of Nazareth as our Lord and Savior. We are together plunged into the mystery of his death and resurrection. In his Spirit, we share one life together which is the very life of God. It is no empty slogan that we are one in the Spirit. This is a profound reality which is being revealed to us in these days . . .

"Finally, I think we have to acknowledge the uniqueness of our time. Has there ever been an age in which the Lord, moving by the power of His Spirit, has done precisely the same thing among all his people divided as they may be? Today the graces of the Charismatic Renewal are searching through every corner of the universal church. Catholics, Orthodox, Protestant and Pentecostal are still divided, hostile, suspicious of each other. Yet in each of our churches and at the same time, the Lord is calling us to deeper conversion, to open ourselves to the continuous outpouring of his Spirit, to receive and use the gifts and ministries of his Spirit, and to live together in submission to each other with meekness, patience and forgiveness so that his Body may be effectively formed. This movement of grace simply cannot be confined to Catholic, Protestant, or Orthodox categories. God is moving among all his people. His movement is bigger and more powerful than we can imagine. What is the Lord's plan? Certainly he is moving in our history, preparing his people by the renewal of his Spirit to be his witnesses. If his purposes match the uniqueness and power of his present methods among us, then surely we are on the verge of an era of total renewal throughout the Church and of a uniquely effective witness in the world." [18]

This breath of Pentecost, which blows at will across the frontiers created by our divisions, is felt not only among us Catholics. It is easy to find testimony to the same experience in other Churches. I would like to close this chapter by quoting these lines from Pastor G. Appia.

Having described his experience with Charismatic prayer groups, he continues:

"Although the road ahead of these brethren is fraught with dangers, from within and without, yet what we see with our own eyes can be considered an awakening the like of which has never been seen before in the history of the Church. To blind ourselves to this would be today, for those of us who are traditional believers, blatant infidelity. It is the Lord who is challenging us at the deepest level of our faith. If, fifty years ago, the first pentecostal communities were quickly pushed out to the periphery of the traditional Churches (for reasons that are easy to detect), and thus often took on the characteristics of a sect, this is not the case today . . .

"All the evidence points to the fact that those who are touched by this reality today wish to remain in the Church and continue to share in the sacraments. They have no desire to fall into some sort of "elitism" of initiates which inevitably leads to spiritual pride . . .

"We should quite simply keep in mind, that once again the truth of this axiom is verified in our midst: each time the Church, the Body of Christ, is exposed to dangers which threaten its existence and its witness, the Lord shows to it signs of his watchful and unwearying mercy. He gives to the Church what it needs, so that it may reveal him and continue its service for the glory of God and the salvation of men.

"It is permissible to surmise that what Pope John XXIII prayed for and expressed as his wish at the opening of the Council is happening here and now. Nor is it an exaggeration to apply to the Charismatic Movement his words: 'a new Pentecost.' " [19]

The Holy Spirit and Mary

Do not be afraid to take
Mary home with you as your wife.
It is by the Holy Spirit that
She has conceived this Child.
MATTHEW I, 20

I. THE HOLY SPIRIT OR MARY?

The period after the Council has been a time of considerable lessening of appreciation for Mary, if not among the
faithful in general, at least in intellectual circles. There was
a reaction against a Marian theology which was too
essentialist, deductive, abstract, and concentrated on her
privileges in a context that was not Christological. This
reaction was opposed to a Marian devotion that remained
on the edge of liturgical renewal, was too dependent upon
private revelations, and too remote from biblical theology.
Besides, at the Council, a concern for ecumenism, which
was always in the thoughts of the Fathers, meant that
stress tended to be laid on what is common to all
Christians: expressions likely to give rise to controversy
were "played down."

All this has resulted in a climate which, if not opposed to Mary, at least shows restraint where she is concerned. And, as always when there is a reaction, we have not been spared exaggerations in the other direction. Now we have to recover our lost balance and see Mary in the Mission assigned to her by God.

I think therefore that there is a real need today, to stress again Mary's role in the perspective of the Holy Spirit. I am convinced that Marian devotion will come to life in the proportion that it is linked to the Holy Spirit and lived under his guidance. Mary will then appear as the one upon whom the Spirit showered his graces, as the first Christian, the first charismatic.

To see more clearly the place of Mary within our new awareness of the Spirit, we should, first of all, take account of what, in her regard, has had an adverse influence on our Protestant brethren.

Many Protestants are of the opinion that Catholics fail to appreciate the role of the Holy Spirit, and therefore the role of Christ as the unique mediator in the Christian life. Without a doubt some of their reticence has been caused by certain exaggerations on our side on the level of theology or popular devotions. Nevertheless, it seems that their greatest uneasiness rests in the fact that they view us as attributing to Mary what, in their eyes, is proper to the Holy Spirit. Some, at least, seem to think that we have put Mary practically in the place of the Spirit. This is a genuine obstacle to ecumenical dialogue and blocks the road to unity.

This difficulty of reaching mutual understanding on the respective roles of the Holy Spirit and Mary has been brought out well by Elsie Gibson in an article entitled, "Mary and the Protestant Mind."

"It is possibly as difficult for Catholics to understand what Protestants believe about the Holy Spirit as it is for Protestants

to understand what Catholics believe about Mary. When I first began reading Catholic periodicals and books, I was puzzled and offended by caricatures of our views regarding the Holy Spirit, more than by anything else. The Catholic consensus seemed to be that we glorify human impulses and judgments, attributing them to the inspiration of the Third Person of the Trinity. This is a travesty of the Protestant position . . .
"When I began the study of Catholic theology, every place I expected to find an exposition of the doctrine of the Holy Spirit, I found Mary. What Protestants universally attribute to the action of the Holy Spirit was attributed to Mary." [1]

More than one fellow Christian feels uneasy when confronted with some of the habitual expressions we use in her regard. Much of this language, in their opinion, suffers from a common fault: it substitutes Mary for the Holy Spirit. We seem to them to attribute to Mary what in fact belongs to the Spirit, or at least belongs to the Spirit in a unique and fundamental way. They point out as particularly shocking, such expressions as:

– To Jesus through Mary.
– Mary forms Christ in us.
– Mary is the link between Christ and ourselves.
– Mary is associated with the act of redemption.

When faced with such formulas, our Protestant brethren object that it is precisely the Holy Spirit who is to bring us to Jesus, to form Christ in us, to unite us to him and to cooperate in a unique way in the work of redemption. This uneasiness of theirs ought to help us to be conscious of the necessary hierarchy of truths in revelation and to reserve for the Holy Spirit his special primary role. We can, then, apply these expressions to Mary in a correct but secondary, derived sense, always in dependence on the Holy Spirit. In any case, the reproach that we have substituted

Mary for the Holy Spirit, or that we have eclipsed his unique and divine role, should not leave us indifferent. We should stop and think. What is more, this reaction is found not only among Protestants, but also among certain Orthodox writers.[2]

Historically, in the Latin Church, Mariology took a great step forward at that time when pneumatology was on the wane. This has had its consequences in our efforts to maintain a doctrinal balance. Elsie Gibson, in the article we have already cited, searches for a way out of the impasse after presenting the two points of view.

"Within Protestantism, this divine Presence (of the Holy Spirit) is recognized by the holiness engendered, whether this be in personality, forms of action, or developments in Church life. Does the Catholic, perhaps, finding these effects more visible in Mary than anywhere else, glorify the Holy Spirit by praising what has been accomplished in her?

"If Mary's life is a first fruit of an anticipatory abiding action of the Holy Spirit in the Church, in contrast to the temporary activity of the Spirit of the Lord in prophetic utterance in the Old Testament, this might help to explain to Protestants the priority given to her in the Catholic Church. Perhaps the Schema on the Church will make the relationship of the Holy Spirit to Mary more clear. But as the matter has stood in the past, here again, the human has appeared to eclipse the divine Person." [3]

These lines can serve as an introduction to a new dialogue. We also believe we should first of all set in relief the absolute priority of the Holy Spirit, the Sanctifying Spirit. Then, having done this, we should reflect upon Mary as the one who, beyond all others, has been sanctified, the daughter of Sion visited by the Spirit, who, moreover, in her response to the angel showed herself to be moved by the Spirit at a depth unique to herself. The faith with which Mary received the offer of God is itself a special act of the Spirit in her. He is the source of all faith. Mary's free and active collaboration was permeated and sustained by the Spirit who worked in her "both the will and the action" (Phil. 2, 13). She remained totally receptive to his action in the very movement of her free response. Mary does not take the initiative: it is the Spirit who invites her and gives her the grace of surrendering totally to him. God's sovereign freedom shines forth in Mary; in her are realized uniquely the wonderful words of Maurice Zundel:

> "God really gives what he gives,
> He still gives what he asks,
> He gives twice what he receives."

The consideration of what the Spirit has performed in the mystery of Mary's life, seems to me a way of lessening or even removing many misunderstandings. But this is just the first point to make. We should go on to show the role Mary, the mother of Jesus and our mother, has in the household of the Church. When family relationships break down, it is natural that reconciliation take place around the mother.

MARY AND ECUMENISM.

Mary's role in our ecumenical efforts has been appreciated in a particular way by a man who was an Anglican and became a Catholic while retaining and widening his friendships among both groups: Martin Gillett. His was the daring idea of transforming what seemed "an obstacle" into a means of approach to unity. This he did by forming an ecumenical movement that took Mary as its starting point. There was no question of theological conflicts, but of peaceful meetings and discussions with the aim of getting to know and to revere Mary more.

This idea first came to Martin Gillett on the occasion of

the fortieth anniversary of the "Malines Conversations" instituted by Cardinal Mercier in the years 1921–26—the first ecumenical exchanges between Anglican and Catholic theologians—in October 1966. During the reception, held at Malines for members of the Anglican delegation who had come to set up a commemorative plaque, he made his suggestion. It was a project in keeping with the spirit of Cardinal Mercier, and it quickly won support among Christians of different traditions.

The first international congress was held in London in April, 1971. I had the privilege—and it gave me great joy—of delivering the opening address on the theme, "The Holy Spirit and Mary," and of meeting Catholic and Anglican bishops as well as representatives of the Ortho-dox and Reformed Churches. From then on, ecumenical Marian meetings continued to be held on many levels in an atmosphere of prayer and mutual exchange. We can only hope that this movement will extend outside England. We mention it here as being full of promise for the future.

Speaking at the world council of theologians held in Brussels in September, 1970, under the auspices of *Concilium*, I stressed the bond between Mary and ecumenism:

"I have no more idea than you do when the hour of restored unity will come. Probably Christians of my generation are destined, like Moses, to view the Promised Land only from afar. However, if I read the signs of the times correctly, that hour is drawing near. The star which led the wise men to Bethlehem is shining in the sky. Pilgrims in search of unity are already on their way. Once in a while, the star disappears and they have to check their route on the map. But the indications are that Bethlehem is close . . . Perhaps our pilgrims, like the magi before them, will first find the mother, and then the child. It is hard to imagine a homecoming of children long separated from one another, without envisaging a mother to welcome them at the door and take them to the Lord.[4]

II. MARY LED BY THE SPIRIT.

The life of Mary, and her role, are contained in the words which determine her vocation as the Mother of God: "The Holy Spirit will come upon you and the power of the Most High will overshadow you" (Lk. 1, 35). We have need of no other text to see Mary's place in the history of salvation. As Alexander Schmemann, an Orthodox theologian, has written:

"To use a somewhat paradoxical approach, I would say that if nothing else were revealed in the Gospel than the mere fact of Mary's existence, i.e., that Christ, God and man, had a mother and that her name was Mary, it would have been enough for the Church to love her, to think of her relationship with her Son, and to draw theological conclusions from this contemplation. Thus, there is no need for additional or special revelations; Mary is a self-evident and essential 'dimension' of the Gospel itself." [5]

At the moment of the Annunciation, the prelude to the Incarnation and Christ's unique role of mediator, Mary was the point of intersection between heaven and earth. We can say that the Holy Spirit is God's love reaching out to us without limit; he is the Envoy of the Father and the Son. On our side, Mary is the love, in its purest form, of a creature who is only a creature, but lifted up by this same Spirit to encounter him. At the converging point of their mutual tenderness, at the very heart of this convenant we find the Christ, our Saviour. We are, indeed, speaking here in halting words: but we are touching upon the very heart of the mystery that is the Incarnation.

Mary's relation to her Son is founded on her motherhood, but, it is as any motherhood, which extends far beyond the bearing of a child in the natural, biological sense. Even on the purely natural plane, does not being a mother imply an interpersonal relationship—the correlative of being a son? Does not this relationship imply an unconditional—and thus definitive—consent to the child's existence as gift to the world? Motherhood cannot be reduced simply to the biological fact of giving birth. The mother consents at first as a whole and then more and more in detail, to the personal existence and thus to the vocation of her child. What is unique to Mary, is the fact that her child is the Saviour of the World. In freely consenting to enable Christ to be present in the world and in history, Mary is also consenting to cooperate in the salvation of the world.

Mary's openness to the Spirit was not limited to the moment of the Annunciation: she remained open and submissive to his action—to his mysterious and hidden power. The Son born of her is and remains the Son of the Father and the Son of Mary. The Spirit is given to her in a covenant that does not belong merely to a moment in time. It is contemporaneous with each stage of Christ's Incarnation.

Because the Christ of faith and the Jesus of history are one, we can say—if we ponder deeply on the mystery of the Incarnation—that Mary remains the mother of the Saviour, the mother of the Incarnate Word, and was affirmed at the Council of Ephesus (431). The graces that we receive today, since they derive from the humanity of her Son, still remain implied in that *fiat* which she uttered to God under the impulse of the Holy Spirit.

Mary's faith did not remain on the level of her initial response. It grew through the darkness of the Cross into the light of the Resurrection.

Our relationship to the *fiat* of Mary, is not only a thing of the past, it remains an actual and personal reality. To receive grace in the Holy Spirit through the mediation of Christ, in his humanity, implies, without doubt, a relationship to Mary's *fiat*. It also implies a relationship with Mary as she now is, filled with this same Spirit, in glory, and directing her gaze toward the Father through her Son. To believe in the communion of saints is to believe that the humanity of Christ remains the source of all grace, and that the history of salvation is not something purely of the past. This means that we have a relationship with all those who have had a role in the history of our salvation—one which is still being continued in the glory that now is theirs.

We cannot isolate Mary in this communion of saints. If we believe in the Church triumphant, then we know that the saints live in Christ in communion with one another and with us. There is relationship, interaction, and reciprocity, each one sharing in proportion to the degree of his vocation and his election. Mary, the mother of Christ, cannot fail to have a unique role in this communion that unites the redeemed around the throne of the Lamb. She remains forever the one who received the Word of God and enabled him to become one of ourselves. She is the link; faithful to the Spirit, she lived to the full, in her soul and body, "the fellowship of the Holy Spirit."

Scripture calls attention to the presence of Mary on Calvary, at the decisive hour of Jesus' redemptive death: "Near the cross of Jesus stood his mother . . ." (Jn. 19, 25). This explicit mention of her presence is full of significance, but I did not need it to know that the covenant sealed by the Spirit encompassed all the mysteries of her Son: joyful, sorrowful, and glorious and that the Spirit is forever the seal of their unity.

And this is not a seal stamped from the outside, like a mark on a document to authenticate it. The action of the Spirit and Mary's action which is totally dependent on and subordinate to the Spirit, tend to the same goal: to give and reveal to the world Jesus Christ, and thus to glorify the Father.

The Spirit is entirely "Christ-bearing." He makes the

presence of Jesus a reality and forms him in us. Only he can enable us to pronounce the name of Jesus for salvation. He enables us to be born to a new life, and gives us the power to live as genuine Christians to the glory of the Father.

As a creature, called by grace to share in the work of the Holy Spirit, Mary is also totally turned toward her Son. She reveals the depths of her own being in the single command of hers that the Scripture records for us. And, again, there is no need of a text to see into the soul which is revealed in the words spoken to the servants at Cana: "Do whatever he tells you" (Jn. 2, 5). Mary's historical role in the past and her mystical role in the present coalesce in this vital relationship with her Son. Mary cannot fail to lead us to Jesus, even as a river leads to the sea; she can only be understood in total transparency in her relation to Jesus. She gives Jesus to us by her own joyous response to him. Christ is the Word made flesh, Mary's vocation is to be the bearer of that Word: she only lives to bring Christ to the world. She is in Christ and for Christ to a depth we cannot plumb. She exists purely in relation to Christ:

> "Now to that face which most resembles Christ
> Lift up thy gaze; its radiance alone
> Can grant to thee the power to look on Christ." [6]

Mary is not a screen concealing the Lord from us. Our hesitation in loving her for fear this will detract from our loving the Lord, derives from a basic misunderstanding of who she is. We are here at the heart of God's mystery. His work is not limited by our categories of time and space: in him we enter in a world of mutual openness, selflessness, communion.

The Spirit who fills Mary is and will always be, the Spirit of the Son. It is the Spirit who "Christianized" Mary at a depth beyond our understanding. She is the Christian *par excellence,* filled to overflowing with the Spirit of Christ. In Mary, the Holy Spirit has created his master-piece: she is his pride, his glory.

> "Woman! above all women glorified,
> Our tainted nature's solitary boast." [7]

Mary's role is not in the order of bestowing grace. The Spirit alone is and remains the Envoy of the Father and the Son. Her place is not as a mediator. Mary's role is in relation to our response. In union with her and following in her steps, we are helped to receive the Holy Spirit and to listen to his promptings. Already enjoying the glory of heaven, she encourages us to continue on our way in confidence and joy. The Council called her "a sign of sure hope and solace for the pilgrim People of God." [8]

MARY, OUR MOTHER IN THE SPIRIT.

In St. Matthew's Gospel, the first message that comes down from heaven to earth is an invitation to receive Mary: "Joseph, son of David, do not be afraid to take Mary home with you as your wife. It is by the Holy Spirit that she conceived the child" (Mt. 1, 20). Apart from the actual circumstances of that moment, this message is addressed to all generations of Christians. To be receptive to the spiritual motherhood of Mary, is an unfailing sign of our openness to the Holy Spirit. This may appear an astonishing statement, yet it is confirmed by experience in the lives of many saints.

In his famous *Treatise on True Devotion to Mary,* St. Louis Marie de Montfort has written some outstanding pages about the relationship between the Holy Spirit and Mary. The saint's theological formulations may surprise us—his wording derived from the period in which he lived—but we are indebted to him for a spiritual experi-ence that has been the source of much grace. In Chapter

IV, we spoke of the experience of God in general. One could also speak of the experience of God as lived by the saints. God, and God alone, is wonderful in his saints. Those saints who "received Mary"—some of whom knew a mystical experience of union with her—witness to the spiritual motherhood of Mary as an operative reality in their lives. Theologians could reflect more on this witness.

Such an experience, which is the fruit of grace, presupposes human cooperation. To experience communion with the Holy Spirit in union with Mary, we must begin by performing some acts which explicitly direct our attention to her. Then there will come a moment when our gaze will be fixed entirely on the Spirit who is forming Christ in us. These first steps call to mind someone learning to drive. At first, he has to think out, in detail, precisely what he must do, beginning with how to put the key in the ignition. Little by little, these actions become reflexes and it becomes possible, at one and the same time, to admire the scenery, talk to a friend, and still be on the alert to use the clutch and the brake. In theory, this sounds complicated. Experience, however, shows that it is really quite simple. All these things go together in an easy harmony. A living union with Mary is like that. We breathe in Mary and breathe out the Spirit. The end in view is always the same: to give Jesus to the world.

This experience admits of degrees, but it is available to all and has a part in the normal development of a Christian life. There are some traits by which we can recognize the presence of the Spirit received in union with Mary. I will confine myself to three. To accept Mary's role as mother guarantees humanity, humility and balance.

MARY AS A GUARANTEE OF HUMANITY.

First let us consider our relationship to Jesus. No one can accept Mary without fully embracing the mystery of the Incarnation. She saves us from any touch of docetism; the heresy which taught that Jesus only appeared to be a man, as distinct from being a human being in the full sense of the word. Mary prevents us from confusing Incarnation and theophany—this latter being a passing manifestation of God. She also keeps us from deism, from the uni-personal God of the philosophers, and thus leads us into the mystery of the Trinity. The reality of Mary is a safeguard against any attempt to keep God at a distance by denying his closeness to us—by denying the mystery of Emmanuel, the unique Son of God in our midst.

Mary is also the guarantee of humanity in the Church and in the world. She is a woman and a mother; and, like all mothers, she has a sense for the uniqueness of each person. She has an instinct for what is concrete, practical, in touch with life. An Arab proverb runs, "Men see the forest, women see the trees and their leaves." In the same way, Mary treats each Christian as an individual. She brings a human touch to technology and the struggle for life. It is difficult to imagine that women, if their political role had been greater, could have callously let loose the barbarous destruction of life during the wars we have seen in our time. In the Church too, Mary, by her presence, can soften the rigidity of institutions and bureaucracies, that anonymity of structures which so weighs on us, even if, in part, it is inevitable.

After Jesus, the Son of God and the most human of men, Mary, his mother, is the most human creature, who ever lived. She is the mother of men in all the dimensions of their humanity. At moments of distress she comes to the rescue. At Cana, she, a mother, was the one to notice: "They have no wine." Here is the complete reverse of the kind of piety that seeks to cut off the "religious" from the "profane" or isolate it in some sublime irrelevance. Grignon de Montfort writes: "She is good, she is tender. There is nothing about her that is austere and forbidding;

nothing too sublime and too brilliant. In seeing her, we see our nature undefiled." [9] This is the opposite of false pride and self-sufficiency.

MARY AS A GUARANTEE OF HUMILITY.

Often people intentionally put the emphasis on Christ, as a reaction against devotion to Mary. Christ, they say, must remain at the center of a religion which proclaims his message, and devotion to Mary can be a threat. This is correct in so far as Jesus must remain at the heart of the Christian life. But this would no longer be so, if Christ were to be deprived of an essential dimension of his being: Jesus is the Son of the Father, but he is also the Son of Mary. Even in the glory of heaven, he remains both. This should be enough in itself to prevent us from thinking of Mary as merely a kind of gateway through which her Son once passed—Mary as someone who can now be cast aside as far as the work is concerned which he has to accomplish for our Salvation. We must not forget that Jesus willed, in absolute freedom, to be dependent upon his mother, not only during the months that she carried him in her womb, but also during the long years of preparation for his public ministry. This fact alone speaks more loudly than all the texts: it contains a whole Marian theology. It encourages us to enter the Kingdom of God by the way pointed out by Jesus: "Let the children come to me. For it is to such as these that the Kingdom of God belongs" (Mk. 10, 14). Mary is the guarantee of the humility of those who rely on her to make them more receptive to the Holy Spirit.

MARY, GUARANTEE OF BALANCE AND WISDOM.

The Incarnation, which is the heart of Christianity, is a mystery of balance and harmony between the divine and the human. Mary belongs to this mystery. We call upon her, rightly, as the "Seat of Wisdom." Her presence can preserve, in an authentic Christianity, a sense of reserve and discretion in regard to the awesome wonders of interventions that come from God.

Visited by an angel, favoured by the most direct experience of God himself, she nonetheless remained humbly and calmly in possession of herself. She simply asked: "How can this come about?" (Lk. 1, 34). There was no exaggeration, no trace of illuminism.

And after that wondrous visit, she went off quietly to help her cousin Elizabeth. When she was greeted with the words: "Blessed are you among women," she prophesied that "all generations will call me blessed," and that included ours. But she did not forget to recall her poverty as a humble servant of the Lord (Lk. 1, 42. 48).

I think that a living perception and recognition of the role of Mary is particularly important in a movement such as the Charismatic Renewal. In the midst of all the extraordinary outpouring of the gifts of the Spirit, it is necessary to maintain a healthy balance and penetrating discernment. The extraordinary, the dramatic, cannot be the norm of life, nor should it make us forget the essential. On the face of it, one might fear that the accent placed on the Holy Spirit within the Renewal, would lessen or cause people to forget the role of Mary. All the more so when one remembers that the classical Pentecostal tradition has not been favorable to devotion to Mary: Catholics, it could be objected, might imbibe this attitude through a sort of osmosis. It was a happy surprise and a joy when, during my homily at the International Catholic Charismatic Conference in 1973, my brief mention stressing the role of Mary as a secret of holiness was met with a standing ovation from some twenty thousand persons. This sincere reaction, coupled with the faith and the joy displayed by that assembly, made me feel we were one family, gathered in our home, around our mother.

I recaptured there something of the atmosphere of the first Pentecost when, in the upper room of Jerusalem, "all were joined in continuous prayer, together with several women, including Mary the mother of Jesus and with his brothers" (Acts 1, 14). At the Congress of South Bend I felt once again how Mary is close to the workings of the Spirit, Mary, mother of Jesus, illuminated by the Spirit as the first charismatic.

As Father George Montague, editor of the *Catholic Biblical Quarterly* has written: "The experience of Mary, is one of the most precious gifts of the Spirit. She is a charism of the Spirit in person. From her I learn to believe more purely, to discern the Spirit more clearly, to listen to the Word more intently, and to await more creatively the hour of the Lord's coming." [10]

The Holy Spirit: My Hope

May the God of Hope fill you with
all joy and peace by your faith in him;
until, by the power of the Holy Spirit,
you overflow with hope.
ROMANS 15, 13

TO PROCLAIM HOPE.

When St. Peter told the early Christians that they should
"have an answer ready for people who ask you the reason
for the hope that you have" (1 Pt. 3, 15), he was not
addressing himself only to the communities, but also to
each individual.

This invitation, therefore, is addressed to me. I have to
profess my hope personally, as I profess my faith. I feel
bound to speak aloud some of the things that have passed
between God and myself. This is not easy. To compose a
spiritual testament is alright, but on one condition . . .
that it is to be read after death!

Furthermore, I would not be truly obedient to St.
Peter's words if I were content to give anonymous or
general reasons for my hope. I shall take the risk then.
And, in faith, I shall bear witness to the Holy Spirit, my
living hope.

My faith in him was not born yesterday. When I

became a bishop, I chose for my personal motto, and as a program for my minstry, the words, *"In Spiritu Sancto"*: "In the Holy Spirit." That was in 1945, surely "in tempore non suspecto"—in an unexpected time. I made this choice because I wanted to commit myself to following, to the best of my powers, the promptings of the Holy Spirit, and to be faithful to his action, both within myself and in the world, no matter what the cost.

Earlier, I quoted the testimony of forty Jesuits who, in the course of their lives, had encountered the Charismatic Renewal and through it experienced what one might call a "re-conversion" as it were, to Jesus Christ and a new openness to the Holy Spirit. Obviously, this experience was not unrelated to their earlier spiritual life, nor was it a technical bolt out of the blue, as on the road to Damascus. But they had been gripped by the Spirit and the Spirit had left its mark upon them. I was tempted simply to quote their witness, so as to avoid the embarrassment of giving a testimony of my own. But that would have been to choose the easy way out, to evade responsibility. So, then, I will take my turn, and tell an experience that is my own.

THE DARK NIGHT OF HOPE.

I will not retrace the whole story of the Spirit's action in me during all those years. To give a true picture, I would have to dwell on my refusals and hesitations to correspond with this grace. But I want to recount here what, for me, was the dark night not of faith, but of hope, which I lived during the period following the Council. I think that almost all the bishops, each in his own way, experienced something like that, when they returned home at the end of Vatican II, despite the joy in their hearts at the thought the renewal was now to begin.

Already during the Council, this very real joy had for me moments of shadow, because of tensions and half-measures that prevented the full realisation of my hopes. But all in all, the balance sheet had been favourable. The positive prevailed over the negative, inviting a mood of euphoria.

Then, after the Council, to the surprise of all, a desolate, devastating wind buffeted the Church of God. A Good Friday began; it was the time of the "Death of God," the denial of Jesus as the unique Son of God, the refusal to accept the Church as the sacrament of salvation. At the same time, a tidal wave of immorality swept through the world: the mass media brought into the limelight the moral decadence of our age and a permissive society reacted not at all, while all too many Christians, by saying nothing, lent their support, so anxious were they to appear broad-minded.

Every local Church knew its trials. With heavy heart I watched many priests, and men and women who had entered religious life, abandon their vocations. The conversations that I had with some were deeply painful: breaks of this kind hurt a lot and leave their scars.

There were other reasons for sadness:

- The constant and worldwide lessening of religious practice since the Council.
- The disturbing drop in vocations.
- The closing of seminaries and novitiates.
- Deeply Christian parents seeing their grown-up children break with the Church.
- Family prayer in many homes completely disappearing.
- Christians totally confused by changes following upon the Council.

The list could go on. However, I will add here, on a personal note, the feeling of solitude suffered by anyone who sets out alone to do what he truly believes to be for the good of the Church: the many misunderstandings, the misinterpretations of motives, the fabrications that would take a lifetime to refute. Then, too, for the bishops of my country, and for me in particular, since my position obliged me to be involved in a special way, the confusion, and the conflicting accusations, when for political reasons, the University of Louvain had to be split in two. This indeed for many years was a Way of the Cross.

HOPING AGAINST HOPE.

I call these things to mind, without dwelling on them in their entirety, to give an idea of the desolation which, humanly speaking, was enough to quench all hope. Were we not, as we continued on our way, like the disciples who on the road to Emmaus, a few days after the crucifixion, said to one another of the Messiah: "We had hoped that he would be the one to set Israel free; and now two whole days have passed since all these things happened . . ." (Lk. 24, 21).

We have re-lived in the Church of today, our Lord's crucifixion, his abandonment on the Cross: "My God, my God, why have you forsaken me?" (Mk. 15, 34). We know by experience the mystery of his agony that has been suffered down the centuries, by his disciples who make up, in their lives, "all that still has to be undergone by Christ for the sake of his Body, the Church" (Col. 1, 24). And yet, I can say that the words of the Lord, "My yoke is easy and my burden light," have always remained for me luminous, like a rainbow in the sky. Never did the Lord fail to make good for me his promise: "You are sad now, but I shall see you again, and your hearts will be full of joy" (Jn. 16, 22). What a strange paradox in our lives is this mixture of pain and joy. Jesus did not promise his own that they would not suffer, he promised a serenity beyond human reach because it has its source in him.

For anyone who asks me the secret of this theological

hope—this hope against hope—I have no answer other than that of St. Paul: "I know in whom I have believed" (2 Tm. 1, 12). Hope grows out of faith, like a flower from a stem. And faith assures me that God is with us until the end of time, and never more close than when the darkness of Golgotha hides him from our eyes.

I believe in the sun even when night or fog covers the earth. I know that the sun is there, true to itself, that its light and its warmth will pierce the clouds. I believe in the sun in the depth of winter. My hope kept alive by faith, assures me of his presence: that is enough. But I also know that in spring the rays of the sun are brighter and warmer. And it is of this springtime of hope that I shall speak now.

A NEW HOPE.

The difference between the winter sun and that of spring is not so much on the side of the sun, but depends upon the position of the earth. I can say, personally, that my hope in God, which was always light to me, like an *aurora borealis,* is now undergoing a change. It is becoming a hope that I experience. It is still the same hope, but there is a freshness in it, a more brilliant light, a more intense warmth. This is because I can see signs telling me that the winter of the post-Council era is evolving into spring, into a rebirth full of promises.

I will not enumerate all these signs: no one can count or classify the rays of the sun, and besides, the action of the Holy Spirit reaches far beyond our field of vision. The Spirit gives life to the Church: he is at work at the heart of the world. No one can write the story of the working of the Spirit, any more than that of Jesus himself, of whom we read at the end of St. John's Gospel: "There were many other things that Jesus did; if all these were to be written down, the world itself, I believe, would not contain all that would have to be written" (Jn. 21, 25).

In describing this new spring, I will limit myself to things that are within my own field of vision. I will confine my testimony to recounting the grace that the discovery of the Charismatic Renewal has been for me. It is a discovery I have made in many countries. And here at home, it is before my eyes and in my heart.

I did not discover the Holy Spirit through the Renewal. As I have said, the Spirit had long been at the center of my life. But the Renewal gave new life to my faith in the Spirit. This is what I mean: I saw how some Christians live, who took the Acts of the Apostles at its word, and this led me to question the depth and the genuineness of my own faith. As a result, I found that I believed in the action of the Holy Spirit, but in a limited sphere; in me the Spirit could not call forth from the organ all the melody he wished; some of the pipes did not function, because they had not been used.

I could have discovered this without the Renewal. Anyone can read the Acts of the Apostles and letters of St. Paul, and then, by way of contrast with what he sees in himself, make an examination of conscience. However, the Renewal enabled me to see the beginnings of the Church in a new light and gave me a living example of that same faith for which I shall always be grateful.

It was a lesson in Christian realism, and I have tried to put it into practice in my life. Without being able to estimate all I owe to other movements of grace in the Church—and my debt is great—I can say, I think, that I owe to the Renewal a spiritual youth, as it were, a more tangible hope, and the joy of seeing impossible things become possible.

OPENNESS TO GOD:
THE SPIRIT REVEALS JESUS AS PERSON.

The God of my faith is the living God, the Father, Son and Holy Spirit. From early youth, I have firmly believed in their mysterious, life-giving presence. But—and this is new—I experienced at a deeper level a need of the Spirit to enlighten for me the face of the Lord Jesus and to create with him a deeper intimacy. And I realised better that the face of Jesus is indeed the face of the unique Son of God.

I said that the surest sign of the Renewal's authenticity rests in its Christology. In proclaiming "Jesus is Lord," Charismatics affirm that Jesus is Son of God in a unique manner, and it thus distinguishes itself from countless "back to Jesus" movements which often present us with a purely human Jesus. Such a Jesus is not the Jesus of my faith "born of the Holy Spirit and the Virgin Mary."

I knew that the Holy Spirit has but one mission also for me: that of revealing the Son to me and in the Son the Father. Thus, it is natural that, under the guidance of the Spirit, the knowledge of Jesus should become more and more personal: I knew this before. But I have now come to a clearer realization that Christianity is not an "ism," but a Someone. And that Someone is the living Jesus. At the same time, I felt—and this indeed was a grace—that I was being asked to open myself ever more to him, in a readiness for prayer. And prayer is becoming more and more a listening: to hear his voice, look upon his face. The words in the psalm had come alive for me: "My heart has said of you, 'seek his face'" (Ps. 27, 8). The Spirit, by revealing this face ever more clearly, is granting in some way a new epiphany.

THE SPIRIT REVEALS JESUS AS WORD.

The Spirit also reveals more intensely for me Jesus as the Word. Of course, I had read the Scriptures and tried through the writings of biblical scholars, to grasp the meaning of the text. This kind of reading will always be indispensable. But there is a reading of another kind, in the light of the Holy Spirit. I open the Bible and the words

I see before me take on a special meaning, as if the Lord has made them the "Word of Life" for me. The Renewal helps me to open the Bible often in the day and to read it with a new taste and a new expectation. It is a communion with the Word of Jesus, as I am, in another way, in communion with him in his Eucharist. His light illumines my darkness. Sometimes the "light" lasts but a moment, as when one turns on an automatic switch in a dark corridor. I am discovering that the Holy Spirit will give—if we ask for it—the lesson in exegesis that Jesus gave one evening to two of his disciples when, "starting with Moses and the prophets, he explained to them the passages throughout the scriptures that were about himself" (Lk. 24, 27).

And his teaching is filled with the light and warmth which led the disciples at Emmaus to say, "Did not our hearts burn within us as he talked to us on the road and explained the scriptures to us?" (Lk. 24, 32). Many people bear witness to the fact that, following upon their spiritual experience of Renewal, the Bible has become for them a spring of living water. I can only add my testimony to theirs.

THE SPIRIT REVEALING HIS FULL
CHARISMATIC DIMENSION.

I have come to understand the Holy Spirit better: I believed already in the charisms of the Holy Spirit, but some of these were scarcely ever used in the daily life of the Church, or in my life. The Renewal, by awakening my faith in the Spirit at work in all his charisms, without exception, compelled me to ask myself some precise questions. Did I really expect that even today the Spirit would speak and act through the charisms of prophecy, healing, interpretation and miracles? Of course, I repeat, a charism of discernment is needed if we are to recognize these gifts of the Spirit. My temptation is to be so much "on my guard" that these gifts are reduced to the sphere of mere possibilities. I have still a long way to go if I am to accept, in practice, that God loves me in unexpected ways, that he invites me to walk on the waters. Nevertheless I am discovering that God is nearer than I thought, that a charism is a manifestation of his glorious love—the love he feels for me and wishes to reveal through me.

I found too, that I did not realize our Lord's promise that his disciples would do greater works than he, because he was going to the Father and would send his Spirit (Jn. 14, 12). I did not really believe that the charisms of the Spirit are always there, today no less than yesterday: they will not be ineffective if I learn to receive them and make them bear fruit in a living active faith.

OPENNESS TO OTHERS.

Openness to God helps us to be open to others in prayer and in life. Experience of Charismatic prayer meetings or a celebration of the Eucharist in which elements of this kind of prayer were integrated, showed me to what degree my usual prayer had remained individualistic. The presence of others close to me on these occasions, murmuring spontaneous prayers, at first annoyed me. A neighbor praying in an undertone irritated me and disturbed "my" recollection. It took some time to learn that prayer can be both deeply personal and yet part of a "symphony." I had to learn too, how to make my own the rhythm and prayer of another. To pray together in this way is completely different from repeating together a "ready-made" prayer. I began to understand the freedom of God's children in the presence of the Lord. This does not mean that we should not observe and respect at the same time the traditional norms for the liturgy . . . but let us keep to the point.

When I had learned to pray spontaneously in a group, I found myself doing so at other times. I might be receiving a visitor or presiding at a meeting. At first, it is a little embarrassing: I still need courage to ask someone to pray with me, perhaps to open the Bible together and pray to the Lord for light. As I began to do this, whether it was to ask for guidance on a decision we had to take, or simply to praise and thank God together, I felt shy and awkward. Only an act of faith in the presence of Jesus in our midst—more real than ourselves—made this possible for me. Imagine our synods or councils if prayer of this kind were woven into the work we do together; if, instead of prayer being merely a preface to the business of the day, it were the warp and woof of our discussions. I still remember a session at Ann Arbor, attended by some fifty delegates. Many times during the meeting, the layman who presided, interrupted our deliberations to suggest a few minutes of prayer and recollection before the Lord, to ask for the light of the Holy Spirit on the decisions we were about to make. This prayer in which we took part together—sometimes a murmur, sometimes for a moment "in tongues"—plunged me deeply into an atmosphere of awareness of God. And I thought: how far we are from believing what we profess to believe!

When I first attended Charismatic meetings, I was struck by the freedom with which people expressed themselves in prayer, even in an exterior symbolic way. Some lifted up their hands from time to time. Sometimes, at the end of the meeting, they prayed with a member of the group who had asked for this, laying their hands on his head as they stood gathered around him.

This occasional laying on of hands is, clearly, not in the nature of a sacrament. This gesture, which is more traditional in the Church than is realized, was, I learned, simply an expression of union with the person for whom and with whom one is praying. As to the lifting up of hands, in the manner of a priest at the altar, this is an external expression of a movement of soul. When I first

met this way of praying—one totally unfamiliar to me—I
felt I had to question my own demeanour. So habituated
are we—and I especially—to control our emotions and
conceal anything that might reveal what is going on inside
us. Timidity, human respect, inhibitions, the education we
have received: all this conditions us to assume a mask of
reserve. We are ready to pray with our soul, but not with
our body. The young know nothing of our complexes, and
express themselves much more freely. As I thought about
this, I came to the conclusion that, in fact, we repress our
natural spontaneity and put in its place a rigidity which
stifles all religious expression. Do we not sing to the Holy
Spirit: *"Riga quod est aridum,"* "Water what is dry . . ."
"Flecte quod is rigidum," "Bend what is rigid." Well then,
let us not be surprised . . . if he answers us!

Of late, when praying I have paid more attention to the
psalms in our breviary:

> "Your love is better than life itself;
> my lips will recite your praise;
> all my life I will bless you,
> in your name lift up my hands;
> my soul will feast most richly,
> on my lips a song of joy and,
> in my mouth, praise" (Ps. 62, 5–6).

There are many such verses to be found in the Old
Testament. We consider it natural that love and friendship
should find expression in outward gestures, but in our
relations with God, we are strangely stiff. Some of my
friends tell me I have become more open, more warm,
more joyful in my day to day contact with others. I do not
know. I leave it to them to judge. I do know that freedom
in prayer, bringing about renunciation of self, greatly
helps to make one genuinely free to express one's feelings
to others. Theology tells me I have no cause to be
surprised: the Holy Spirit, by definition is openness,

receptivity, bond of union; everything that encourages better human relations is fruit of his presence.

But this is only one aspect of things. Viewed from within, this spiritual Renewal is not an isolated grace, cut off from the context of our lives. It intensifies all the sacramental graces already received, which meant for me the sacraments of initiation as well as the episcopal consecration. For me, it was as if all those previous sacramental graces gathered into one, were working within me.

In asking a group of friends to pray for me, and in receiving their fraternal gesture of solidarity as they laid hands on me and prayed that I be more and more faithful to the Holy Spirit, I was carrying out, I reflected, St. Paul's injunction to Timothy: "That is why I am reminding you now to fan into a flame the gift that God gave you when I laid my hands on you. God's gift was not a spirit of timidity, but the Spirit of power, and love and self control" (2 Tm. 1, 6–7).

To give a true picture of my reactions to the Charismatic Renewal, I have to say that I had to face a number of doctrinal questions. First of all, I had to disassociate it from a vocabulary and theology which had their origins in classical Pentecostalism. This helped me to understand better the meaning of the gifts and the charisms, their role and their limitations. In particular, I had to clarify in my own mind the exact meaning of "speaking in tongues" and healing. In the course of this book, I have shared the result of my reflections. There are other problems too: theological and pastoral. Research must continue: theologians and spiritual leaders have here an important service to render. Pope Paul VI has already urged us to pursue more thoroughly studies in the sphere of pneumatology. But if we wish really to understand such manifestations of God, then we must study them from the inside, on the basis of

personal experience and with humble readiness to learn
from and benefit by the experience of others.

CONCLUSION.

These thoughts have not been easy to put into words:
we cannot express in human language the workings of
God in the depths of our hearts: we easily confuse the
human and the divine. Only Mary in the Magnificat was
able to sing the marvels that the Lord worked in her, and
in a tone befitting a pure transparency before God.

Such as they are, in all their inadequacy, these words
wish to say one thing: the Lord is near, God is not dead,
Jesus is alive, the Spirit is faithful; in the heart of our
twentieth century, Pentecost remains a reality.

I wrote these pages having in mind all who, in the
Church, have need for a renewal of hope. I offer them to
priests and lay people, and to my brother bishops who will
be called more and more to exercise a role of discernment.
John XXIII and Paul VI have not prayed in vain for a new
Pentecost. It is here, before our eyes, like the first rays of
dawn. But it cannot shine in all its splendor unless we can
recognize it and accept it in all its consequences. We are
living in a moment of grace: God respects our liberty and
will not force the door; but he is knocking! As the
disciples at Emmaus, let us learn to recognize the Lord as
he walks at our side. Let us pray to him: "Stay with us, for
evening draws on and the day is almost over" (Lk. 24, 29).

A journalist thinking of the last Synod, asked me the
other day: "What do you think constitutes at the present
time the greatest obstacle to the evangelization of the
world?" Without hesitation I answered: "The lack of faith
among Christians as to what, by the grace of God, they
really are." I know that evangelization of the world is a
term which includes many realities and demands a variety
of approaches. Grace does not destroy nature: it embraces

human reality—its contours and complexities. But by the power of God it carries this nature infinitely beyond itself.

We have to respect differences in vocation: "There are many rooms in my Father's house" (Jn. 14, 2), but the foundation of the house is one. No matter what our individual vocation and our field of action may be, we have to give the best of ourselves, that is, Christ within us, acting by the power of the Holy Spirit. Herein lies the salvation of the world.

It is essential that our faith should grow deeper, that we Christians can face the world of today and bring to it the Gospel. "The love of Christ constrains us" Paul said (2 Cor. 5, 14). We are called upon to enkindle the fire of Christ's love in a world that is in danger, in a Church that is suffering.

Some time ago, I composed a prayer for the people of my diocese. It is a prayer of hope, and I offer it to the readers of this book, asking them to be one with me in a communion of faith, hope and love.

Prayer

Give us, oh Lord,
eyes for seeing,
a heart for loving,
breath for living.

Give us eyes for seeing,

give us, we beg, your eyes,
to see through them
the world and all mankind,
to see their history and our own
as you see them.
Grant us to think your thoughts
day by day,
hour by hour.
Help us gradually to become

that for which you created us;
let us adopt your view of things,
your way of seeing things.
Make us responsive to your Word
which can enlighten and transform
the life of each of us.

Give us a heart for loving,

a heart of flesh and not of stone
for loving God and Man.
Give us, we beg, your heart,
that we forget ourselves
in perfect love.
We need to exchange our heart for yours,
our heart so slow
to love all others but ourselves.
Let it be you, oh Lord,
who loves through us.
Give us a heart to love Our Father,
to love Mary our Mother
and to love your brothers
who are also ours;
to love even in this world
those who have gone before us in the next—
to love also those
who walk beside us
here on earth
and who sometimes
are more difficult to love.

Give us the breath of life

that our lungs be constantly filled
with life-saving breath and air
to help us walk towards tomorrow
without a backward look or thought of effort;
to prepare for
all that men, and therefore you,

expect from us;
to draw fresh hope
as if, this morning, life began;
to struggle against winds and tides,
sustained
by your presence and your promise,
carrying as we do, in us,
mens' hopes and all their fears.
Give us breath to live, your breath
that you send from God the Father;
your Spirit, the Breath
that blows where it will;
in gusts or sudden winds
or that light touch
with which you call us to follow.
Breathe on us,
inspire in us
that prayer which rises from you within us,
calling for you to come in glory,
reaching out to the fullness of God.

Lord, I need your eyes,
give me a living faith.
I need your heart,
a love to withstand any test.
I need the breath of God,
give your hope
to me and all your Church
that the Church today
bear witness to the world,
that the world may know
all Christians,
by their look of joy and serenity,
a warm and generous heart
and the unfailing optimism
that rises
from that secret, everlasting spring
of joyful hope.

Epilogue

The Spirit remains at the heart of the Church, directing us towards the future. We would like to have a glimpse of that future, so as to read better the signs of the time. But this is not essential: our hope for the future is not based on statistics and charts. It derives entirely from faith in the Spirit, who is with the Church as it moves into the future.

The Spirit is the living breath of the Church, leading it on its pilgrimage, as long ago the pillar of cloud by day, and of fire by night, led the people of Israel in the desert. He is at once continuity and freshness: "things new and old" (Mt. 13, 52); tradition and progress.

TRADITION.

A living Tradition, the Spirit unites all successive generations to the Lord Jesus "who is, who was, and who is to come" (Rev. 1, 4). He makes clear those things in their Master's teaching that the disciples of Jesus were not then able to bear. Little by little, he heals their "incredulity and obstinacy" (Mk. 16, 14). He draws from the one word of God the water which will quench the thirst of each generation: "You will draw water joyfully from the springs of salvation" (Is. 12, 3). He calls to mind the Word of God, giving to it a freshness and a power to shed light on what is happening at the very moment. He does not repeat himself: each time his teaching of the Word has a new resonance, a new urgency. Left to ourselves we have only the text of the Gospel: if we are to understand its true, living message, the Spirit must bring it alive.

PROGRESS.

The Spirit is also a Spirit of progress, reaching out to what is to come, carrying the past, to direct it into the future. He influences the great decisions that have, in the past, determined the course of the Church's mission. The Acts of the Apostles speaks of his presence at the Council of Jerusalem (Acts 15, 28), and attributes to him Paul's decision to cross into Europe (Acts 16, 6). The Spirit unceasingly prevents the Church from taking itself as an end in itself, from indulging in self-satisfaction. He wants Christians to set out on their journey afresh each morning, taking as little baggage as possible. "The Church," the Patriarch Athenagoras said: "is not the Kingdom of God; it is the sacrament of the Kingdom." [1]

A ready openness toward the future is an integral part of Christianity. The end of time is not simply an unveiling, the drawing back of a curtain: it is a promise which must find its fulfilment in the future. Christian time is dynamic openness to the future and to God who is with us on our way. It is the mission of the Holy Spirit to carry the hope of this future. At certain moments, the Church has felt itself in a mysterious way, thrust forward by the Spirit. The present time offers us a grace: it should find us attentive and open. As Henri Gouhier said, "Nothing greater ever happens in history than a change in hope." We are now living amid just such a change. The Church of tomorrow, if it is faithful to its call, will be, like the God of hope who, as Peguy said, is "both young and eternal." We must not fear the unknown ways of God, nor the renewals needed if the Church is to keep young.

We have to accept as a message for our times, the words of Isaiah, the prophet:

> "Remember not the former things,
> nor consider the things of old.
> Behold, I am doing a new thing;

now it springs forth, do you not perceive it?
I will make a way in the wilderness,
rivers in the desert. . . ." (Is. 43, 18–19).

*   *   *

PENTECOST CONTINUES. . .

Notes

PREFACE

1. Constitution *On the Church*, par. 4.
2. *Pensées*, 14.
3. H. Caffarel, "Il n'en faut pas plus à Dieu" in *La Chambre Haute* 2, pp. 33-34. (*La Chambre Haute* is a bulletin for prayer groups of the French language published by Editions du Feuy Nouveau, Paris.)
4. As reported in the journal *Avenire*, January 12, 1969.
5. See *The Critic* Vol. 29, No. 2 (November–December, 1970).

CHAPTER I

1. General Audience, June 6, 1973.
2. Quoted in *Le Monde*, July 19, 1973.
3. Address to Participants in second Congress of Canon Law Sept. 17, 1973. *Oss. Rom.* (Eng. ed.) Oct. 4, 1973, p. 12.
4. Allocution to the Curia, Sept. 21, 1962. *The Pope Speaks*, 9 (1963) p. 154.
5. "Mutation religieuse et renouvellement theologique" in *Revue théologique de Louvain*, 4 (1973) pp. 296-297.
6. In O. Clément, *Dialogues avec le Patriarche Athénagoras* (Paris: Fayard, 1969) p. 154.
7. General Audience of July 9, 1969. *The Pope Speaks*, 4 (1969) p. 95.
8. A. Schmemann, "On Mariology in Orthodoxy" in *Marian Library Studies*, 1 (1970) pp. 25-32.
9. "Main Theme Address" in *The Uppsala Report 1968* (Official Report of the Fourth Assembly of the World Council of Churches, Uppsala, July 4-20, 1968), Geneva, 1969 p. 298.

CHAPTER II

1. In the article on *Pneuma, Theological Dictionary of the New Testament* (Eng. Tr. G. Bromiley: Grand Rapids: Eerdmans, 1969), VI.
2. L. Cerfaux, *La communauté apostolique* (Paris: Cerf, 1956) pp. 13-14.
3. *Against Heresies*, 5, 6, 1.
4. Constitution *On the Church*, par. 12.
5. Decree *On The Apostolate of the Laity*, par. 3.

CHAPTER III

1. Paul Evdokimov, "L'Esprit-Saint et l'Eglise d'après la tradition liturgique" in *L'Esprit-Saint et l'Eglise*, published by l'Académie internationale des sciences religieuses (Paris: Fayard, 1969) pp. 94–95.
2. *On the Ministry and Life of Priests*, par. 5. The Latin of this remarkable phrase runs, *"per Carnem suam Spiritu Sancto vivificatam et vivificantem."*
3. See the article by J. Mambrino, " 'Les deux mains de Dieu' dans l'oeuvre de saint Irénée," *Nouvelle Revue Théologique* 79 (1957) pp. 355–370.
4. Quoted by P. Evdokimov in *L'Esprit-Saint dans la Tradition Orthodoxe* (Paris, 1969) p. 98.
5. The *epiclesis* of the Liturgy of St John Chrysostom, translated from the *Ieratikon* (Rome, 1950) pp. 134–135.
6. These lines are taken from a fragment of his work, *Against Fabianus*. See *Patrologia Latina*, Volume 65, columns 789–791.
7. J. M. R. Tillard, O.P., "L'Eucharistie et le Saint-Esprit," *Nouvelle Revue Théologique* 90 (1968). See pp. 372–373.
8. This text, and the following liturgical texts, are taken from the material published by the Canadian Catholic Conference. In every case where there is an official English translation, the text they give will correspond to it. For this text, see *The National Bulletin* on the *Liturgy*, Number 26 (March 1969).
9. Cf. the Liturgy of the Paschal Vigil—the Missal.
10. See the *National Bulletin on the Liturgy*, No. 37 (January, 1973) p. 106.
11. In his treatise *On the Baptism of Christ*, see *Patrologica Graeca*, Volume 46, column 581.
12. See the *National Bulletin on the Liturgy*, Number 37, (January, 1973) p. 51.
13. *Ibid.* p. 49.
14. This prayer and the following formula are taken from the booklet, *Pastoral Care of the Sick and the Rite of Anointing*. English translation of the rite is that of the International Committee on English in the Liturgy.
15. From the Apostolic Constitution, *Sacrament of the Anointing of the Sick*. Confer the booklet referred to in note 12, p. 11.
16. From the article cited in note 1, p. 88.
17. For a study of some aspects of what is called inner healing, and the sacraments, see F. Martin, "The Healing of Memories," *Review for Religious* 32 (1973)/498–507. Also, M. Scanlon, *The Power in Penance* (Ave Maria Press, 1973) pp. 498–507.
18. Though studies in areas of healing and prayer are necessarily tentative, and though I cannot agree with every detail of them, there are two particularly valuable books that could be mentioned

here: Agnes Sanford, *The Healing Gifts of the Spirit* (Philadelphia, 1966); Francis McNutt, O.P., *Healing* (Notre Dame, 1974).

19. *Sacramentary 1973–1974.* Approved by the National Office for Liturgy for use in the Churches of Canada (G.C.C. Publications Service, 1973).
20. *Mysterium Salutis,* (Einsiedeln, 1965).

CHAPTER IV

1. Jean Mouroux, *L'expérience chrétienne, Introduction à une théologie* (Paris, 1952), p. 5.
2. G. Huyghe, *Elise d'Arras,* 22 (1972) pp. 641–642.
3. Mouroux, *op. cit.,* p. 6.
4. There is an interesting note on page 8 of Mouroux's book which refers to an article by Gregoire, "Notes sur les termes 'intuition et experience'" in *Revue philosophique de Louvain* 44 (1946) pp. 411–415. Mouroux sums up the article this way: "The author gives the word four different meanings—verification, knowledge drawn from life, experimentation, habitual knowledge. 'The common element is an immediate knowledge of concrete things', and 'ultimately, the word *experience* suggests concrete knowledge and knowledge united to life.'"
5. One could consult for example, *Summa Theologica* II–II, 1, 2; esp. ad *2um*.
6. See the article by Kilian McDonnell, O.S.B., "I Believe that I Might Experience" in *Continuum* 5 (1968) pp. 673–685.
7. R. A. Knox, *Enthusiasm: A Chapter in the History of Religion* (5th ed. Oxford, 1962).
8. *The Undistorted Image: Staretz Silouan,* 1866–1938. Ed. by Archimandrite Sofrony (London, 1958) p. 81.

CHAPTER V

1. In the article on *Pneuma, Theological Dictionary of the New Testament* (Eng. Tr. G. Bromiley: Grand Rapids: Eerdmans, 1969), VI.
2. K. and D. Ranaghan, *Catholic Pentecostals* (New York, 1969).
3. E. O'Connor, C.S.C., *The Pentecostal Movement in the Catholic Church* (Notre Dame, Indiana, 1971).
4. An interesting account of this weekend can be found in *New Covenant,* Vol. 2, No. 8 (February, 1973).
5. Ranaghans, *op. cit.,* p. 7.
6. D. Wilkerson, *The Cross and the Switchblade* (18th printing, New York, 1970).
7. Ranaghans, *op. cit.,* p. 20.
8. G. Kosicki, C.S.B., *The Lord is My Shepherd, The Witness of Priests* (Ann Arbor, 1973).

9. "The Pentecostal Thing and the Jesuits," in *Studies in the Spirituality of Jesuits* 5 (June, 1973). This periodical is not sold to the public. All the citations in this section are taken from the early pages (pp. 113–120) of the study.

10. There are many useful studies that treat of the difficult exegetical problems raised here. Among these studies we could name: S. Tugwell, O.P., *Did You Receive the Spirit?* (London, 1972); James D. G. Dunn, *Baptism in the Holy Spirit* (Studies in Biblical Theology) (London, 1970); F. D. Brunner, *A Theology of the Holy Spirit*—The Baptismal Text of John 3, 5," in the collection of articles: I. de la Potterie, S. Lyonnet, *The Christian Lives by the Spirit* (Eng. Trans. New York, 1970) pp. 1–36.
articles; I. de la Potterie, S. Lyonnet, *The Christian Lives by the Spirit* (Eng. Trans. New York, 1970) pp. 1–36.

11. F. A. Sullivan, "Baptism in the Holy Spirit", *Gregorianum* 55 (1974), p. 4.

12. The passage is found in *Summa Theologica* I, 43, 5, ad *2um*. The references to St. Augustine used by St. Thomas are: *De Trinitate* 9, 10; and 4, 5.

13. This quote is found in the article which follows that cited above, therefore: *Summa Theol.* I, 43, 6, ad *2um*.

Chapter VI

1. Address to the College of Cardinals, Dec. 21, 1973. *The Pope Speaks* 18 (1973) p. 334.

2. Publications Office, U.S. Catholic Conference (Washington, 1973).

3. *New Covenant* Vol. 3, No. 5 (Dec. 1973) p. 5.

4. William J. Samarin, *Tongues of Men and Angels* (New York, 1972).

5. See especially, *New Covenant* Vol. 2, Nos. 4 and 5 (Oct. and Nov. 1972).

6. I have developed some aspects of this question in an article "What Can We Do to Overcome Unnecessary Polarizations in the Church?" *Concilium* No. 88 (New York, October 1973) pp. 119–122.

7. This comparison is to be found in a study which has not yet been made public. I am grateful to Father McDonnell for letting me use it here.

8. T. S. Eliot, "Little Gidding" in *Collected Poems: 1909–1962* (London, 1963) p. 222.

9. Steve Clark, *Where Are We Headed?* (Ann Arbor, 1973) pp. 16–20.

10. In *America*, June 16, 1973, p. 551.

Chapter VII

1. Bishop G. Huyghe, *L'Eglise d'Arras*, 1973, No. 2.

2. *"Fiunt, non nascuntur christiani,"* Apology, Corpus Scriptorum Ecclesiasticorum Latinorum, Vol. 69, p. 46.
3. K. Rahner, "The Christian of the Future" in *Convergence* 6 (1965) pp. 3–4.

CHAPTER VIII

1. Stephen B. Clark, *Building Christian Communities: Strategy for Renewing the Church* (Notre Dame, 1972) p. 10.
2. L. Bouyer, *L'Eglise de Dieu* (Paris, 1970) p. 336.
3. The three most important "summary statements" in the Acts of the Apostles are: Acts 2,42–47; 4,32–35; 5,12–16. These are passages in which St. Luke sums up, as it were, whole aspects of the early community's life.
4. See 1 Pt. 2,17; 5,9.
5. S. Clark, *Building Christian Community, op. cit.,* pp. 33, 40, 43.
6. Translator's note. I am going to use the term "basic community" throughout this section to translate the French *"Communauté de base."* Unfortunately we have no consistent English equivalent of this phrase so common today in languages deriving from Latin. The reference is to new communities; we call them under this aspect "experimental." As they are not religious, we call them "lay communities"; and since they usually do not have a form of life as yet fixed by a constitution, we call them "unstructured." They are often composed of men and women, usually including married couples and celibates; for both reasons we call them "mixed." They are most often quite restricted in size; thus we speak of "small communities." As the ensuing discussion will make clear it is the quality of life and faith of these communities, rather than any of their particular characteristics, that merit for them the name Christian. Some of these characteristics are, however, a true faith response to a movement of the Spirit. A good discussion of some aspects of "basic communities" can be found in the book by Fr. Max Delespesse, *The Church Community, Leaven and Life Style* (Eng. Trans. Ottawa, 1968).
7. D. Bonhoeffer, *Life Together* (Eng. Trans. New York, 1954) p. 26.
8. D. Bonhoeffer.
9. K. Ranaghan, *The Lord, The Spirit and the Church* (Notre Dame, 1973) pp. 52–53.
10. G. Pulkingham, *Gathered For Power* (New York, 1973); M. Harper, *A New Way of Living* (New Jersey, 1973).
11. J. Randall, *In God's Providence*, New York, 1973.
12. L. Rétif, "Paroisses et unités de base" in *La Croix*, Mar. 15, 1973.
13. J. H. Newman, *Lectures on the Present Position of Catholics in England: Addresses to the Brothers of the Oratory* (Dublin 1857), p. 359.

14. For information about the Focolarini, and a sense of their spirituality, it is helpful to read some of the writings of Chiara Lubich herself: *That All Men Be One*, (New York, 1969); *When I Love in Charity* (New York, 1972), etc. There is also Pierre Raffin's article, "Spiritual Revival and Renewal in the Religious Life" in *Concilium*, No. 89 (New York, 1973) p. 139.
15. Constitution *On the Church in the Modern World*, par. 11.
16. *Osservatore Romano* (Eng. ed.) Mar. 28, 1974.
17. *Wind, Sand and Stars* (Time-Life Books, 1965) p. 245.

CHAPTER IX

1. In *Le Monde*, July 19, 1973.
2. R. Garaudy, *Reconquête de l'espoir* (Grasset, 1971) pp. 135–136.
3. In *Eglise de Grenoble*, May 31, 1973.
4. Marcel Legaut, "La passion de l'Eglise," *Etudes*, No. 333 (October, 1970) p. 425.
5. R. Haughton, "Signs of the Times," *Catholic World*, No. 211 (September, 1970) p. 246.

CHAPTER X

1. *The London Times*, January 18, 1973.
2. There is a good discussion of the importance of this statement in the article by the Lutheran theologian, V. Vajta, "L'Avenir de l'oecumenisme," *Nouvelle Revue Thélogique*, 95 (1973) p. 996.
3. See, for instance, the Report of the Lutheran-Roman Catholic Study Commission on "The Gospel and the Church." The text can be found in *Worship*, 46 (1972) pp. 326–351.
4. H. Ryan, "The Canterbury Statement on Ministry and Ordination," *Worship*, 48 (1974) pp. 12–13.
5. Address to the participants in a meeting held by the Vatican Secretariat for Non-Christians. *Osservatore Romano*, Oct. 6, 1972.
6. *The Catholic Herald*, November 24, 1972.
7. See the article by E. Lanne, O.S.B., "Le mystère de l'Eglise et de son unité" in *Irenikon*, 46 (1973) pp. 298–342; especially pp. 301–311.
8. I have developed this in a talk given in the American Episcopal Church in Paris, May 8, 1971. See *Documentations Catholiques*, 68 (1971) pp. 674–678.
9. The text can be found in *Diakonia*, 8 (1973) pp. 291–300.
10. This text is also reported in *Diakonia, vol. cit.*, pp. 386–390.
11. *La Croix*, October 13, 1973.
12. One could consult in this regard the article by D. J. Constantelos, "Theological Considerations for the Social Ethos of the Orthodox Church," *Journal of Ecumenical Studies*, 11 (1974) pp. 25–44.
13. From a statement made in New York, January, 1972.

14. *La Croix*, March 4, 1972.
15. *On Divine Revelation*, par. 10.
16. Constitution *On the Church*, par. 4.
17. *New Covenant*, Vol. 4, No. 1 (July, 1974) p. 5.
18. K. Ranaghan, *The Lord, the Spirit and the Church*, (Notre Dame, 1973) pp. 11–12; 16–17.
19. G. Appia, "Une nouvelle Pentecôte," *Unité Chrétienne* 28 (November, 1972) pp. 55–56.

CHAPTER XI

1. E. Gibson, "Mary and the Protestant Mind," *Review for Religious*, 24 (1965), pp. 396–397.
2. For some further study on this point, one could consult: R. Laurentin, "Esprit-Saint et théologie mariale," *Nouvelle Revue Théologique*, 89 (1967) pp. 26–27; B. L. Marchand, "Le contenu évangélique de la dévotion mariale," *Foi et Vie* (1951) p. 517; P. Pare, "The Doctrine of the Holy Spirit in the Western Church," *Theology* (1958) p. 297.
3. *Art. cit.*, p. 397.
4. The full text can be found in *Pastoralia*, 20 (October, 1970).
5. A. Schmemann, "On Mariology in Orthodoxy," *Marian Library*, *1* (1970) pp. 25–32.
6. Dante, *Divine Comedy*, Paradise, canto 32,85. (Eng. Trans., Penguin Books, 1962).
7. W. Wordsworth, "Sonnet to the Virgin."
8. Constitution *On the Church*, par. 68.
9. G. de Montfort, *True Devotion to Mary* (Eng. Trans. F. W. Faber, New York, 1949) p. 62.
10. G. Montague S.M., *Riding the Wind* (Ann Arbor, 1974) p. 98.

CHAPTER XII

1. O. Clément, *Dialogues avec le Patriarche Athénagoras* (Paris, 1969), p. 136.